Jen!
Always be happy +
love yourself first!
Love
Paul J. Meredith

Is it ANY Wonder You're Single!

Is it ANY Wonder You're Single!

*Everything you wish you knew about landing **MR. RIGHT***

PAUL J. MEREDITH

BIG BEAK PUBLISHING
TORONTO

Big Beak Publishing
Toronto, Ontario
CANADA

10 9 8 7 6 5 4 3 2 1

Library and Archives Canada Cataloguing in Publication

Meredith, Paul J., 1971-, author
Is it any wonder you're single! : everything you wish
you knew about landing Mr. Right / Paul J. Meredith.

Includes bibliographical references.
ISBN 978-0-9938551-0-8 (pbk.)

1. Mate selection. 2. Dating (Social customs). 3. Man-woman relationships. I. Title.

HQ801.M47 2014 646.7'7 C2014-904834-3

Ordering Information:
Quantity sales. Special discounts are available on quantity purchases by corporations, associations, and others. For details, contact info@pauljmeredith.com.

Table of Contents

ACKNOWLEDGEMENTS

I would first like to thank my very good friend Pete, for spending countless hours reading and rereading this book while providing me with pages and pages of edits. It was a lot of work and for that I can't thank him enough.

Next, I would like to thank my friend Kyla, whose insight was a huge help. Her colorful comments helped to make the editing process all that much more enjoyable for me.

I would also like to thank all the guys that were by my side while learning and studying male/female interaction over the many years of research that went into this book. Mark in particular, who I have been out with many times over the years was an important contributor.

I also can't forget about all the women who both rejected and accepted me over the years. This includes every woman I have ever approached or chased. Those who I just had casual conversations with who refused to give me their number, the ones who were rude, and all the great women I have dated in the past.

I of course can't forget about my beautiful girlfriend Kelly. She helped me to realize the importance of writing this book and how many women I could help by bringing this knowledge to them. She also played a significant role in the final editing of the book.

INTRODUCTION

Women are irrational! At least, that was a thought I had carried around with me for years and is something that most men would agree with if asked. But is it true that women really are irrational? Or is it that men just do not understand women and the way they think? Have you ever wondered what is going through a man's mind when you first meet him? Have you ever scrutinized your thoughts during the early stages of a relationship and really asked yourself if your thoughts are properly guiding you?

There are many thoughts that go through an individual's mind during the first few weeks of a relationship, from the time they first meet until the end of their first date and beyond. Some of these thoughts may be accurate, but many of them are fabricated by our minds to support our limiting and often erroneous beliefs. We will analyze many of the common thoughts men and women have during this period. The objective of this book is to help you understand not only the thought process of men, but also your own thoughts and interpretations. With a clearer understanding of your thoughts, as well as the thoughts of the men you are dating, you will open up a new world for yourself in the way you view your dating habits. By recognizing these thoughts, you will then be able to make a more accurate judgment as to whether they are serving you well. With an understanding of a man's thoughts, you will have a much better idea of whether the guy you are dating is on the same path that you are or whether he is just wasting your time. You will be able to separate the douche bags from the knights in shining armor. You will start to see that there are far more relationship possibilities than you had imagined and in turn, significantly reduce much of the dating frustration you have gone through in the past.

This book is based on personal experience interacting with literally thousands of men and women. I have been studying social interaction between men and women for years, which began with fifteen years of frustration followed by ten plus years of serial dating. On top of the practical experience, I have read countless books written for men, women, and couples. This book is a summary of my findings.

Throughout much of the book, I will be generalizing, so of course this information will not apply to everyone. Some of the information in this book will speak to you while some may not apply at all. You can choose to believe all of what I say or none of it, as I am speaking solely from my own experiences and my interpretation of those experiences. This is what I have come to understand happens in men and women's minds during the initial stages of any relationship, from a guy's perspective.

I ask that you read this book with an open mind, take notes and highlight the parts that speak to you. You deserve the best, and I believe that this book will give you a guide to help you find the man you truly deserve to be with.

Why I wrote this book

I decided to write this book after years of researching and studying male-female social interaction and the psychology related to it. If women were more conscious of certain behavior, they could significantly reduce the amount of men they were dating who were just out to waste their time. This entire process really started to make me love women all that much more. They don't deserve that type of poor treatment from anyone, and, while I am not entirely proud of all my actions in the past, I am thankful for the experience. I can now use this knowledge to help people. If I could help women become more conscious of these patterns, then I could significantly improve their odds of finding that one person they truly deserve to be with so they could stop wasting time! I learned that there are a tremendous amount of great women out there and I am also aware that there is an equal amount of great men out there. All players do is keep them from finding each other. I have found my purpose in life and would like to help as many women as I can find true love and happiness by finding the man they deserve to be with. The great men will thank me for it as well (even if they may not realize my intentions with this book at the time).

Let's get your journey started!

CHAPTER ONE

YOUR JOURNEY BEGINS

"When one door closes, another opens; but we often look so long and so regretfully upon the closed door that we do not see the one which has opened for us."
~Alexander Graham Bell

I still remember my first dating experience clearly. I was fourteen years old on a family vacation to Acapulco. It was here that I met a girl named Christine who was the first girl that I realized actually liked me. I never had the experience to pick up on these signs myself, so I relied on another teenager a few years older than me to let me know what was happening. I took his suggestion and decided to go for a walk on the beach with her that evening, which I didn't realize was probably a pretty stupid idea. After all, it was about 11pm and we were in Mexico of all places. Anyone could have been on that beach, but we were only fourteen and weren't really thinking of any potential consequences.

Nothing happened during that walk other than us talking about our trip, Mexico, back home in Canada and so on. I really wouldn't have known how to make a move, even if I wanted to. I was filled with nervousness as I felt the cool Mexican sand underneath my bare feet, listening to the tranquil sound of the Pacific Ocean waves crashing up on the beach. I really had no clue what to do, so I figured I would just wait for something to happen...and of course, nothing did. As we were walking back, I noticed my Dad standing on the beach up ahead. I knew I was in trouble. I didn't want my parents to know I was walking along the Mexican beach at night with a girl I had just met. Her parents were worried about her and my parents were worried about me. We both got an earful that evening when we returned, which I knew I would never forget. My parents never did offer me up any sort of advice on what I 'should' have done in that situation. I just felt like I made a huge mistake, and this 'in my mind' made it harder for me to take chances with women in the future.

My next experience occurred on a trip to Florida the following year. There I met Jennifer, who 'I thought' was my first love. This was the first girl that made it very clear that she liked me and this was when I discovered the importance of chemistry. I was also getting attention from other girls on that trip and I started to realize that women actually found me attractive after all. Over the next few years, I started to really focus on pursuing women. Little did I know at the time, but this would become a lifestyle over the next twenty years.

I was still completely clueless around women throughout most of my twenties and was confused, shy and frustrated. I just couldn't figure out how I could attract them and overcome my shyness. I never really had much experience with women, or self-confidence for that matter. I started to once again develop a belief that women just didn't like me, despite being told that I was a pretty attractive guy by many girls. I however chose to focus on the negative, which sent me spiraling emotionally downward into the deep and fiery pits of doom. (Okay, so I felt like being overly dramatic!)

I started to forget about my initial success in Florida and was getting depressed. I was really struggling to get a second date, and wondered what was wrong with me (queue the negative self-talk). Even if I managed to make it past the first date and get something started, girls would break up with me after three months, if not sooner. I was stuck in 'The Dating Habit.' It seemed as though I couldn't keep anyone and I didn't understand how different women were from men. I thought if I was thinking a certain way, then she probably was as well. Without having anyone there to actually guide me, I was forced to figure everything out on my own if I wanted to break this cycle. It really wasn't until around the year 2000 when I started internet dating that I started to really begin to learn, and learn fast I did. I immediately started going on about two to three dates per week, studying and learning more and more with every interaction. I was starting to enjoy this process and started thinking less and less about my dream of pursuing a relationship and more and more about just having fun and having sex. The problem was that I was treating many of these women quite unfairly by leading them on. The whole 'nice guy' attitude went right out the window as I began to tell women what they wanted to hear in order to get what I wanted. My lack of self-confidence at the time prevented me from being up-front with my intentions, or flat out lying about them all together. It was a front I was putting on which really wasn't me, however it did get me what I wanted at the time. I became, for lack of a better word, a 'player'.

I wanted more, so I started reading books and going to seminars about picking up women. I was now addicted to learning about them and would spend hours each day on internet forums, studying the material in books, and learning as much as I could about women. I discovered how they think, what attracts them, and how the vast majority of guys just don't seem to get it. I was one of those guys, but I was starting to leave that part of myself behind and began moving forward to a new, better and more confident self. As I was traveling for business at the time, I went out frequently in various cities around the US, trying out different 'lines' and pieces of 'material'. I studied women's reactions to everything. I also would make daily trips to various malls to approach random women to practice everything I was learning. I started to notice patterns in their behavior and realized with the right formula, and the fact that I was starting to become much more comfortable around women, they were becoming a lot easier to pick up.

THE FRAMEWORK OF DATING

There is no question that I encountered my share of frustration along the way. I found myself getting into what I call 'The Dating Habit.' This is where you find that you're always dating and your 'relationships' are never really going anywhere. It seems as though the longer you have been in the dating game, the harder it is to become happy and the more frustrated you become. We go from being single, to meeting someone, dating, then breaking up before we move on to start the cycle again. It's an endless loop of frustration.

When we are stuck in this loop, it can become very difficult to break the cycle that becomes part of our life, and we may even become comfortable with it. Just because you are comfortable with something doesn't mean you are content with it. You might be comfortable with your current job or relationship, but that doesn't mean you are happy with them. Moving on to another job or a new relationship means change and moving into the unknown. Even though it may be the best thing for you and may be what you want, you may hesitate because it would mean moving out of your comfort zone where you are now. This causes fear, doubt and uncertainty.

When we look at it as a sequence and break down each phase, we can better understand and improve the way we navigate through it, therefore increasing our chances of success. It starts from the moment before you meet and goes all the way through until your first date and beyond. You start off as being single and then what happens? Someone spots you, and then they approach. Once you have met, mutual attraction has to be built. Once attraction has been established, there has to be a certain comfort level between the two, which also has to be built. At that point, the two decide they would like to see each other again so they agree to a first date. Then you have that waiting phase in between the meeting and the first date where you don't know what is going to happen. Finally, you get together on the first date where you establish further connection and chemistry. If that goes well, then it moves forward from there. This dating sequence can also be referred to as 'The Game.'

THE DATING SEQUENCE

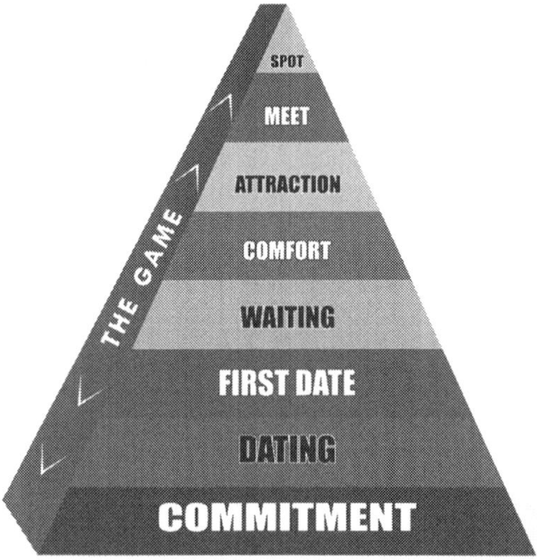

It is referred to as a game, as dating is a challenge, just like a game. There is always strategy that needs to be used in order to give yourself the best chance for success. While no one really likes 'playing games', it doesn't mean going into dating and just letting the chips fall where they may. Otherwise, why even bother to read this book? You want to give yourself and the relationship the highest probability of success. It isn't about 'playing games'. It is about using strategy without having to resort to deceitful or manipulative tactics.

Each phase of this sequence will be explained in detail in chapters six through ten, but here is a brief explanation of what each phase is about:

Spot

You see someone you like and either they approach you or you approach them. This applies to whether you meet them in person, or online. Someone has to take action if you are ever going to meet.

Meet

This is where you make your first impression. The meeting part is simple, as it really only lasts a few seconds. It is a crucial element because nothing else can take place until you meet.

Attraction

Once you have met, a mutual attraction needs to be established. Without attraction, it is unlikely the interaction will progress any further. This is the point where each person is intrigued by the other and wants to know more.

Comfort

This is where you further build your rapport and start to feel more connected with each other through casual conversation. You of course aren't going to want to go any further with someone you don't feel comfortable with, so this phase is one of the most important parts. This is where you realize that there may actually be something here.

Waiting

This is the period where you are in limbo. You are waiting for him to call or text (or wondering if you should text or call) and you don't know if it will actually progress into a first date. This is also the only phase that can be skipped. If you meet someone and hit it off right away, you both may move into the first date immediately after attraction and a small amount of comfort has been established, therefore circumventing the waiting phase all together.

First Date

This is the first meeting where you go deeper into comfort building and get a better idea as to whether there may or may not be a relationship opportunity. You want to determine if the connection you had when you first met can be sustained and improved upon.

Dating

Your first date went well and you start going on more dates together. You are now dating each other, but no exclusivity has been discussed.

Commitment

You both understand that there could be a future together, so you mutually agree to see each other exclusively.

Each phase is a key element and the dating progression cannot happen without each one present (with the exception of waiting, as indicated above). The progression can stop at any part throughout the cycle, so it is important to understand each phase so you know where you stand and how to best navigate through it.

Before we get into the dating sequence in more detail, we will need to look at some of the roadblocks you may be encountering which are holding you back from meeting the right person. The next chapter is dedicated to better understand your struggle to find Mr. Right.

CHAPTER TWO

YOUR STRUGGLE TO FIND MR. RIGHT

"Whenever you want to achieve something, keep your eyes open, concentrate and make sure you know exactly what it is you want. No one can hit their target with their eyes closed."
~Paulo Coelho

I hear women complaining about men all the time. They say things like "there are no good men out there," or "all the good ones are taken." The fact is that there is an ocean of men out there. You just have to recognize and attract the right ones. You go to the mall, you meet with your accountant, your lawyer, your teacher, your classmates, your workmates, people at the grocery store, in the elevator or even walking down the street. Mr. Right could be any of them. With men being ubiquitous, is it really true that there are no good men out there and that they are ALL taken, or is this something that you are telling yourself to justify your being single? Even worse, to justify dating the wrong guy just so you don't have to go through the pain of being single or because your biological clock is ticking? Is it because you are waiting for the 'movie moment'? Are you waiting for the right guy to just drop down from the heavens, sweep you off your feet and make you feel like Cinderella?

Why do you think you are struggling to find the guy you deserve to be with? Do you think it is possible that you could have met him in the past and not know it?

There are many men you encounter in your day-to-day life. They are where you work, where you shop, walking past you on the street, at parties or events you attend. There are possible suitors everywhere. It is just a matter of connecting with them. You may even have single men in your social circle right now that you may not have even considered. "Oh, he's just a friend" you say. But is he really just a friend? Or does he just not know how to make his move and that is the label you have attached to him? Do you think it is possible that you may be discrediting a potential Mr. Right without even realizing it? Perhaps you have in fact met him in the past and told him to get lost because you didn't recognize it was him?

WHY WOULD YOU TELL HIM TO GET LOST?

It is not uncommon for some women to get approached by men frequently, and in many cases, yes, the man is hitting on them (and often poorly at that). Women can be very picky and so they should be. After all, you can't date every... Ahem... loser that approaches you to find out if they may be the one. While some men understand how many times women get approached, others do not.

There are many reasons why a woman might blow off Mr. Right. Sometimes you may be out with your friends and are just having a good time with them and aren't open to meeting new people. He may come across as nervous, shy, or he may say something that you misconstrue. This is something that I find happens frequently and quite often after mutual attraction has already been established. Perhaps you were overly challenging, aloof or even a little bitchy without taking the time to actually find out if this may be the person you are looking for. I will be talking about these points in much more detail in Chapter Seven, but for now, realize that Mr. Right could be anywhere and could approach you at any time. The question is, are you ready for him?

STOP MAKING EXCUSES

Everyone makes excuses and these excuses very often hold us back from what we really want in life. We make up excuses to try to justify why we are overweight, why we haven't found love, why we don't have our dream job, or simply why we are not happy in life. We create these excuses, hide behind them and use them as a type of protection. They can become very real to you because you have been using them for so long they feel comfortable. You are always looking for ways to validate them, yet they victimize you. I used to walk around in search of my perfect match and would find myself discrediting everyone. She's too tall, she's too short, too thin, too wide, hair is too short, hair is too long, not attractive enough, too attractive (that one still shocks me to this day), too old, too young, probably has a boyfriend, probably this, probably that. Blah blah blah blah blah blah blah. You have to know what you want if you are ever going to find it, and it starts by identifying the excuses you use to hold yourself back.

- All the good guys are taken
- Women don't approach men, that's their responsibility (more on this later)
- I'll never meet anyone
- I don't need a man
- I'm too busy
- I have other priorities right now
- I'm not attractive, why would anyone want to date me?
- He's too this, I'm too that, he is probably this, or he is probably that

This list can go on forever, so I would encourage you to come up with a list of the excuses you find you are making and then ask yourself the following question: Are these excuses supporting me and my goals? In most cases, they really won't be. I used to be the excuse KING! I used to say all the time that I couldn't go out to meet women because there were none where I lived and I had to drive too far, couldn't afford to go out, or didn't have the time. I look back at a lot of these now and just laugh. If you put half the energy into finding the right person as you did coming up with excuses, you would have found Mr. Right a long time ago. Stop coming up with excuses just so you can justify why you are still single. **If you were truly going after what you wanted, would you still be making up these same excuses?** That's a serious question.

Take some action...

It is time to take some action to understand your excuse making patterns and to correct your thinking in a way that will support you.

- Take the time right now to write down your top three excuses. Once you have them down, underneath each one write down how each excuse benefits you. Do this now before moving forward.
- Now write down how your life would be different if each excuse was no longer true. It is important to make sure you are completely honest with yourself here. **If you can't be honest with yourself, then how do you expect others to be honest with you?**

The above exercise may not be easy for you, but do yourself a favor and take the time to do it. By gaining some clarity on your excuse making, you can start to work on the areas that are holding you back.

WHAT ARE YOUR STANDARDS?

While it is good to know what you want and to go after it, it is also important that you take a look at your standards to ensure they are realistic. For example, if you are low on the attractiveness scale[1] and you won't settle for anything less than Brad Pitt (not someone that just LOOKS like Brad Pitt, but Brad Pitt himself), then that is a problem. If you are eliminating every dating opportunity that comes your way just because the guy isn't Brad Pitt, then you are (of course) setting yourself up for disappointment and failure. While this is an extreme and ludicrous example, there are some extreme and ludicrous reasons why some women would eliminate otherwise perfect matches for themselves. There is nothing wrong with having high standards, in fact, I encourage it, but it is crucial that they be realistic. If they aren't realistic, then you just bought yourself a one-way ticket to Singleville, population, one. You also need to watch out for the partner and accomplice to having unrealistic high standards, which is having an unrealistic set of rules.

ARE YOUR RULES KEEPING YOU STUCK?

Sarah is looking for Mr. Right and is starting to become frustrated with the fact that she is still single, as it seems like her search has been going on forever. She meets a lot of men and goes out on a lot of dates but just can't seem to find anyone good. She complains time and time again that there aren't any good men out there. The problem is that she has a rule where a guy has to spend a minimum of $150 on their date, and if he doesn't, she takes offense and that is

---

[1] Attractiveness plays a huge role in both men's and women's behavior and how they interact with one another. More on this later

the end of that guy. This is regardless of how close a match they may have been, or how much fun she had on the date. A friend of hers has a $300 rule! Good luck ladies, seriously.

There is nothing wrong with having rules. Just like with having high standards, I encourage having some rules in place as well. The rules I am talking about however are rules that support you in finding what you want. They should be about simple things such as, he must be fun, be employed, and have a good relationship with his family. Rules surrounding values are great, and should be the kind you have. Any other rule you may have should be preferences, rather than hard and fast, do or die, carved in stone kind of rules.

Unrealistic rules become even more apparent in online dating, which is something I have done a lot of over the years. There is one profile that I still remember to this day. It read something like this:

- If you make a daily trip to Starbucks, then don't contact me
- If you have more than $1,000 in debt, not including mortgage and car payment, don't contact me
- If you like to have cereal for breakfast, don't contact me.
- If your name is Dave, Mike, Rick, John, Mark, Jason, Rob, Chris or Steve then don't contact me.

Okay, I just made up the last one to further illustrate my point, and it made me laugh at the same time. It really goes without saying that the woman who wrote the above profile is significantly limiting herself, and something tells me that even if she does find someone that meets the ridiculous set of criteria listed, she will come up with a new set of rules to follow. Needless to say, she will most likely be alone and unhappy for a long time. As long as we are on the subject of making up rules, here's one of my own:

Don't make ridiculous rules!

It's the elusive obvious. Make sure you take a good look at any rules you may have for elimination of potential suitors and ask yourself if they make sense. Always try to look at your rules from an outsider's perspective and don't come up with excuses to justify them. It is important to get out of your head and come at this with an open mind.

I was going out with a couple of my female friends recently and one of them said that she wouldn't date anyone under six-feet tall, which seems to be a fairly common rule for women. I told her that I was five-foot-eleven and was clearly taller than she was, even with heels. "Oh, that's fine!" she responded smiling. This is even a bigger issue online. If you want someone who is six-feet tall and you set your preferences so you won't get messages from anyone shorter, then you could be eliminating a lot of great guys who are five-foot-eleven. Trust me… you won't know the difference between five-foot-eleven and six-feet when they are standing beside you. This is even more important if you are shorter. I can understand you want someone taller, but why should the guy have to tower over you?

Don't discredit a guy because of a height you arbitrarily came up with off the top of your head that simply sounds good to you. It is fine to want someone taller than you are, but they shouldn't have to tower over you either.

SO HOW CAN YOU ATTRACT MORE MEN?

It is important to understand that men are very visual (yes, I know, you have heard this before). While women may be more attracted to the way a man makes them feel, men are more attracted to looks first, the whole package second. In fact, physical attractiveness is the feature most important to us, at least at the beginning. It doesn't mean that we don't look for personality and other positive attributes, but physical attraction is almost always a deal breaker if it isn't there. If the guy is a nine and the girl is a four[1] on the attractiveness scale, it probably won't happen unless the girl brings herself up a couple of notches. If the guy isn't physically attracted then there is little a girl can do unfortunately. As shallow as this sounds, it is the reality of the situation. This may sound a little harsh, but I don't believe in sugar coating anything, as that won't help you. This is one reason why some women get approached all the time, while others get very little attention from men. If you want to get approached more, then it is time to do something about it!

YOU'RE MORE ATTRACTIVE THAN YOU THINK

The good news is that just about everyone can be more attractive (both men and women) if they just put a bit of effort into it. Pay close attention to make up, your hair and

---

[1] Men will attach a number to a woman on a scale of one to ten based on how attractive he thinks she is.

the clothes that you wear. It also doesn't hurt to get your nails done. Buy some fashion magazines, but DON'T compare yourself to the women in the magazines! They are who THEY are and you are who YOU are. You are beautiful in your own way. You are buying the magazines to look for the latest hairstyles, fashion trends, etc. You want to look for clothing that is a little sexy, but not over the top. Avoid any floral patterns. Men simply don't find them particularly alluring. Think in terms of Forever 21, not Forever 75.

If you take a look at many of the women in Hollywood and look through all the make up and glamour, they are fairly average for the most part. Do you really think Paris Hilton is really THAT attractive? I sure don't. Average at best. But she knows how to dress and present herself in a certain way. Women who don't pay that much attention to their looks will have a much harder time meeting and keeping a desirable man.

This applies well into the relationship and after marriage as well. Some women get married and let themselves go. They think that their man has already committed, so they no longer need to put the effort in. Her husband then starts to lose attraction for her and starts noticing other women who ARE putting in more effort. The man may then start to drift, and his chances of cheating are increased.

Just because he has committed to you does not mean you have to let yourself go! Always try to look like a million bucks and keep him chasing after you. Keep the romance alive! Don't let your relationship or marriage start to slide for something that could be easily prevented. You feel so much better about yourself when you look good, so why not look AND feel your best at all times? I digress.

On the other hand, if you are naturally beautiful, then you may even want to tone it down a bit as some men may find this intimidating and won't approach. Or they may approach you for the wrong reason. If you are naturally beautiful, then you may find that you need to put a lot less effort into meeting men. This book, however, isn't about how to get as many men as possible. It's about how to get the right man. So while you may have no problems meeting men, you want to be sure that you develop a strong personality. This way, when the right one does come along, you will be ready to show him you are different from all the others. Looks wear off eventually, so you need to develop a personality that will captivate him for life.

TAKE PRIDE IN THE WAY YOU LOOK

You are a beautiful person, so take pride in the way you look! Put some effort into your appearance and watch for the spike in the self-confidence and self-esteem that inevitably comes with it. Visualize how you would like yourself to look. Have an image in your mind of yourself as the most attractive woman out there. Hold this image in your mind and your body language will start to change making you naturally more appealing. Your mannerisms will start to change, as well as the way you communicate. You will no longer be as concerned with how other women look around you. **Your perception of how you look is even more important than how you actually look** for these very reasons.

If you feel other women are more attractive or better than you, then the reverse also applies. You may not be as friendly and cheerful as you would if this were not a factor.

You owe yourself more than that, and this is something that you can control. Always ensure you look your best when you leave home. I make sure that I look good before walking even ten feet to the garbage chute in my condo building. I am not saying you need to dress as if you are presenting at the Oscars while out walking your little Yorkshire terrier Fifi, but just be conscious of your appearance.

While women may be critical of how they look around each other, we men typically don't give a hoot about what other guys look like around us. As you focus more on yourself you'll forget about other people. How you look at yourself is how others will see you, and that is the only thing that matters!

CREATE APPROACH INVITATIONS

Nothing is going to happen until one person approaches the other. Most men think it is impossible to approach a woman out of the blue without being formally introduced. I had to learn to do this. It wasn't easy and it took a lot of courage the first time I tried it (not to mention, the second, third, fiftieth, hundreth, etc). Ninety-nine times out of one hundred, men aren't going to just come over and approach unless you give them some sort of hint, or approach 'invitation.' By learning how to attract more men, you will have a much larger pool to choose from. This will significantly increase your odds of finding the right one. As it is not at all easy for most men to approach, you need to become more approachable so you can make it a little easier for them. I've already discussed improving your appearance. Now that you have guys swarming over you, here are some simple, yet powerful tools you can easily use to get that fish to strike!

Smile!

Men LOVE it when you smile at them. It makes us feel warm and special inside. There is nothing wrong with this at all as it's innocent and flirtatious. You are not being too 'easy' by smiling. Men don't think that way, so don't even let that enter your mind. We men are just thinking about how we can meet you at this point, and sex is the furthest thing from our minds. We may have sex on our minds a lot, but we certainly don't at that time. We are just thinking about how we can meet you and we don't want to screw it up. If you see someone you like, make strong eye contact and give them a quick (and genuine) smile. Whenever you smile at anyone, they will naturally reciprocate and the more you smile, the more positive reactions you will get!

While walking to the gym this morning, a young woman walked past me with a big smile on her face. She wasn't smiling at me, she just seemed naturally happy. Just seeing her smile immediately made me feel happy. What a great gift she gave me that morning without even realizing it! When people see you with a happy smile, it's contagious and your positive energy will naturally transfer to others.

Do you find you aren't smiling enough? Train those facial muscles so that smiling becomes effortless and natural. You can do this by practicing smiling in the mirror. Yes, you will look uber dorky! Loosen up the smiling muscles in your face and train them to make smiling all that much easier throughout the day. Then, as you go out for the day, try smiling for no reason. Think of something that makes you happy, as your smile will become genuine and powerful so you aren't walking around looking like a jack-o-lantern. It takes seventy-two muscles to frown but only twenty-three to smile. Give others the gift of your smile!

Personality

Are you happy in your life right now? If not, does this have an effect on your actions and how you act around men? Ask yourself this question and it is important that you answer honestly. Would you enjoy being around yourself and being a part of your day-to-day life? Again, answer honestly. If you are looking for honesty in a relationship then being honest with yourself is part of it. By liking who you are, other people will naturally like you more. Your personality will come out and you will be much more fun to be around. This alone will attract more men. Who doesn't want to be around someone who is full of personality?

While your appearance may be the main reason why men approach you initially, it will take a lot more than your looks to hook and keep a quality guy. For starters, are you nice and friendly when they approach? The guy will have a much harder time being himself if you are grumpy or unfriendly. Not to mention he probably won't want to stick around long enough to get to know you. This sounds like it should go without saying, but if the guy looks like someone who you could see yourself with, try being a little friendlier and see what happens. If you are shy but come across as dull and uninteresting, you run a serious risk of turning away Mr. Right. Practice your conversational skills by making small talk with everyone you interact with on a day-to-day basis. Talk to your coworkers, the person beside you on the bus, the cashier at the grocery store. Everyone. It doesn't necessarily have to be interesting conversation, just get into the habit of talking to strangers.

When a man is passionate about things in his life and expresses this passion through emotion and excitement in his voice, he becomes more attractive to women. He becomes more interesting and charismatic. You can do the same by having the same passion when you talk about the things that you love around him.

If you hone your conversational skills every day, you will naturally become more talkative. This makes it far easier for your divine personality to come shining through and will prepare you for when Mr. Right actually does approach...and he will. You are going to knock his socks off (and maybe his pants too)!

Body language

Are you approachable? Is your body language friendly and inviting or is it closed off and turning people away? If you are out somewhere with your friends, are you all standing in a tight circle or sitting around a table in a corner somewhere? While you may get certain men with balls of steel approaching you while seated in a circle with a group of your friends, most likely this won't be the case. Always be conscious of your surroundings. If you are out where men congregate, pay particular attention to your body language and what you are doing. If you are out shopping and you are constantly texting or on your phone, men will not approach. If there are attractive men around you, keep your phone in your purse. You can text your BFF about what happened on the Real Housewives of New Jersey when you are back home. I can't tell you how many times I have been out looking to meet someone and everyone I am interested in is yammering away on their phones. Being aware of your body language increases your chances of getting approached. Again, remember to smile!

Women are typically much better readers of body language than men are[1]. While men aren't necessarily going to notice little incongruencies in your body language, you may have noticed that you do. If a man's words do not match his body language, you will subconsciously take the body language as correct. In fact, women may turn a deaf ear on what is being said altogether. This is how some men can get labeled as being 'creepy', which could also be a lack of self-confidence on their part, or they just may not be comfortable in that situation.

JUST BE YOURSELF?

Probably the most common piece of dating advice given amongst friends is to 'just be yourself', but is that really good advice? What if you aren't happy with who you are? If you have zero self-confidence and are also needy and clingy, do you really want to continue to be that way? What if you are the type of woman that sleeps with everyone on the first date and lets men walk all over you? Are you the type of person that agrees with everything a man says regardless of what it is, just because you want him to like you? If you want to find Mr. Right, you have to be happy with who you are right now, and if you find that you are

---

[1] The Definitive Book of Body Language' by Allan and Barbara Pease

constantly seeking approval then my guess would be you are not. As the old adage says, "If you keep doing what you have always done, you will continue to get what you have always gotten." If you find that what you are doing right now isn't working, then it might be time for a change.

There are a lot of people out there that don't like themselves, and the more you don't like yourself, the lower your self-esteem will be. This directly affects the choices you make. It starts with loving yourself. **If you don't love yourself then how do you expect others to fall in love with you?** Don't confuse loving yourself with being conceited. I am talking about having a solid respect for yourself. If you are truly in love with yourself then watch how quickly you stop worrying about what other people think of you. Start looking for ways to better yourself and watch how your self-confidence and self-esteem will start to improve. This will also have a positive impact on how you interact with your friends and family.

Chapter Two Highlights

- ✓ Stop making excuses
- ✓ Have high standards, but ensure they are realistic
- ✓ Focus on improving physical attractiveness (and anyone can do it!)
- ✓ Your perception of how you look can be more important than how you actually look
- ✓ Be more approachable
- ✓ Smile more

- ✓ Cultivate your personality
- ✓ Be conscious of your body language
- ✓ Love yourself. If you don't love yourself, then look for ways to change so you do!

Now that we have all that handled (and you are working on it, right?), it is time to learn how you are going to recognize Mr. Right so you don't tell him to get lost when you meet him!

CHAPTER THREE

HOW TO RECOGNIZE MR. RIGHT

"When you meet someone better than yourself, turn your thoughts to becoming his equal. When you meet someone not as good as you are, look within and examine your own self."

~Confucius

You hear some people saying that they will 'just know' when they meet the right person, but do you really *just know* about someone when you first meet them? While there are always going to be cases where you are in fact right, most people are rarely themselves when you first meet them. They are either on their best behavior, or are feeling social anxiety, which is not letting them be themselves. So how is it possible you could 'just know' when you aren't even sure who this person really is? Maybe you are thinking that you don't want someone with social anxiety. Fine, I can certainly understand where you are coming from, but let's take a moment and look at social anxiety a little closer.

Close your eyes for a moment. I want you to imagine you see a guy that you would like to meet. At first glance, he looks absolutely perfect for you. Now I want you to imagine walking right up to him. Introduce yourself, make some small talk and then ask him out.

How does this make you feel? Why don't you try it in the real world and see what happens? No? Let me ask you this then… why don't you want to? Is it a fear of rejection? A fear of looking foolish? Are you shy? Too nervous? This is what every guy goes through when they see someone they like and think about approaching them. It is not something that comes easy for most, if not ALL guys. They might be sitting there thinking of the perfect thing to say, or they will make an assumption right away that the woman wouldn't be interested in them or they will envision rejection in some way. The fewer women the guy approaches on a regular basis, the harder this will be for him. Unless you approach guys on a regular basis, you would go through the same thing. It is human nature.

How about if you are already dating someone? I have met many people that have been in a relationship for three or more years and they are still not sure. If you are uncertain at this stage, when will you be certain? How much time do you want to waste? I have met people who say they have 'just known' after only a few weeks. Well, they found out pretty quickly that their 'just knowing' was inaccurate. As I mentioned, people are not themselves when you first meet them, which makes it almost impossible to 'just know' early in the game.

I believe there should be a certain element of 'just knowing', but if a year goes by, and you still aren't sure, then it might be time to start looking for the person that you will be sure about.

DO YOU KNOW WHAT YOU WANT?

I would say many people, both men and women, are not clear on exactly what they want. If I were to tell guys that I suggest that women wait longer before having sex, as it would improve their chances of securing the man of their dreams, they would think I was crazy (more on this later). Just as men aren't always sure of what they want, women can be equally unsure. They will say one thing, but their actions and choices don't support what they think they want.

Do you actually know what you want? The only way to even have a chance of 'just knowing' is to KNOW what you want. **You can't find what you want if you don't have it clearly identified.**

Society influences us and we tend to do what society thinks is right. Most people tend to conform. Just because society says you have to get married, doesn't mean you have to. While this may very well be what you want, do it because it is what YOU want to do, and not what society, your family or your friends think you should do. Be clear that YOU are in control and not anyone else. It's *your* life.

First, you are going to need to be honest with yourself. Honesty is crucial for any relationship to get off the ground properly, yet alone work out in the end. If you can't be honest with yourself, then how are you going to be able to be honest with Mr. Right? This next exercise is crucial in finding the right person, so make sure you focus and are 100% honest with yourself.

Take some action…

Make sure you are in a quiet place where you won't be interrupted before starting this next exercise, as it is a key element in your success. You are serious about finding him, so make sure you take this seriously and do it right.

I want you to start off by describing how it would make you feel and what it would mean to you when you find your perfect match. Go into as much detail as possible on how your life would be.

Now write out EXACTLY what you want in every detail as I indicate below. Make sure you are as detailed as possible for each point. Don't just answer my questions, as I am just giving you ideas.

What does he look like?

Detail is important here, so don't just say he is 6'1" with brown hair and weighs 185 lbs. Go into detail. What type of hair? How long? What style? What is his build like? What is his skin color and tone? Is he the same ethnicity as you? What is his complexion like? What do his legs look like? His hands and feet? What are his teeth like? His lips? What is his body like? Does he workout? How often? Does he have any tattoos? What does his smile look like and how does it make you feel when he smiles at you? What age range?

How does he walk and talk?

Slow? Fast? Is he always in a rush to get places or does he take his time? Is he expressive in his speech? Does he have an accent?

What is his personality like?

Is he outgoing or more introverted? Does he have a sense of humor? What type of sense of humor? Is it dry and sarcastic? A cheesy, stupid sense of humor? Dirty? Does he playfully tease you in a fun and loving way where you can dish it out right back to him? Is he always having fun? Does he have you laughing regularly? What is his temperament like?

What does he do for work and how is he financially?

How often does he work? How much money does he make? Does he have other sources of income as well? Does he have his weekends free? How is he with his money? Is he frugal or spendthrift or somewhere in between?

What is he like sexually?

Does he have a high sex drive or more moderate? What does he like to do and how good is he at it? Is it satisfying? Is he adventurous? Don't be afraid to go into detail here (you can then email me what you wrote….okay, maybe you can just keep it to yourself).

What is your relationship like with him?

Do you communicate with each other? Is he loving towards you? Does he want children? How many? Is he affectionate? Does he fulfill your emotional needs? This is also a good place to mention that you want someone who is 100% committed to you if you are looking for long-term commitment or marriage. Write it all down!

What are his interests?

Does he play sports? If so, how often? Does he watch sports? How often? Does he like the outdoors? Describe what he likes to do outdoors. Does he like food? What type of food? Going out to restaurants? What type of restaurants? Does he eat healthy? Is he into fitness and nutrition? Does he like animals? Is he a dog or a cat person?

Is he religious?

To what extent? Does he go to church every week? Is he of the same faith as you are?

What is his outlook on life?

How does he see the world? Is he always happy? Does he believe in personal development and personal growth? How does he handle any problems you may have?

General qualities

Is he caring? Considerate? Passionate? Good with others?

Charitable? How is he with this family? How is he with children?

Is there anything else you can add? Now is the time!

Great job! If you did this exactly as I specified, you probably were falling in love while you were writing. You are now starting to have a better idea of what you are looking for.

We are not done yet though. Now I want you to write down what your musts are. Which of these qualities MUST he have. This means that if he doesn't have these particular qualities, then it is a deal breaker.

- Must he be employed?
- Must he be sexually satisfying?
- Sense of humor?
- Must have/be/do..... complete the list!

Now make a list of the 'must nots.' List all the qualities that would be deal breakers.

- Smoking?
- Bad attitude?
- Bad breath?
- Drugs?
- Clingy?

Now describe the type of person that he would be attracted to in full detail. Are you this person? Do you see any room for improvement you can make in yourself to better attract him?

Where would he be? Where would you find him? Downtown? At an art gallery? A fund raiser? At a seminar? Go into detail, and dig deep. Now you'll know where to find him.

Read through everything you wrote every single morning before you leave your home. Visualize as you are reading. You should feel like you are falling in love and you should be naturally smiling the entire time.

After I first completed the above exercise, I met my long-term girlfriend Kelly within three days. She had the majority of the qualities I was looking for, or pretty darn close. I have friends who have had similar results as well. Just remember that the 'perfect' man does not exist, and there are always compromises that may need to be made. You can however come close, which is why this exercise is so important. You can't come close if you don't have what you are looking for clearly defined.

Now that you have identified what you want, it is time to look closer at what kind of guy you are attracted to. I'm not going to help you out with ideas this time around. You'll need to pull them from deep inside, and realize they are your thoughts alone. It is important that I don't influence your list in this case. The purpose of this exercise is to ensure that you are very clear on what it is you're looking for, so that you don't waste time with the wrong men. Just like with the previous exercise, be as detailed as possible on what you are attracted to.

Make a list of this now and remember it is crucial that you are honest.

When you compare the two lists, are a lot of the things you are attracted to on the list of what you want? Or do they conflict? Look at the description of your perfect guy again and see if you think you would recognize him when he approaches you, or if you would fluff him off. When reading through your two lists, which one are you more ATTRACTED to? By bringing the two lists into alignment, you give yourself clarity to what you truly want deep down. Make sure who you thought was Mr. Right is actually going to be attractive to you when he approaches!

WHO'S IN CONTROL?

I have found that it is very common for women to be attracted to men who are in control of themselves, do their own thing, and aren't really influenced by what others think. They are attracted to men who can be in control of them, without being controlling. Women will typically not admit this, not even to themselves, but subconsciously, these are the rules they live by. While you may be uttering curse words at me right now, and contemplating throwing this book out the window, give me the benefit of the doubt here for a moment. Women are completely turned off by weak-minded men who give them what they think they want and answer to their beck and call. You know you don't want a guy who is a pushover. You want a guy you can respect. This is why it is so important that the two lists you came up with are in alignment. If they are not, then you will have a problem finding someone you are going to be happy with.

I remember seeing a married couple on an episode of Dr. Phil. The woman had set all the rules for him, including the implementation of a curfew. While she might THINK she likes this control (and clearly the guy has his own issues), it is quite clear that she does not have any respect for him. It is also safe to say that he doesn't have any for himself either.

Some women are just naturally assertive, but they can lose respect for their men if they allow them to take control. These women are sometimes referred to as being bitchy. So why is it that men who are more assertive are considered self-confident while women are bitchy? This is just how society tends to view things. How you view it is really all that matters, but do you really want to be controlling men like this or do you want someone who is going to stand up for himself? Again, make sure you know what you want and then go after it.

Now that you have a clear understanding of what you are looking for and what your deal breakers are, you can come up with a list of questions to ask him on your first date, or possibly even when you first meet him. You will find that you will save yourself a whackload of time. I'll be talking more about what to do when you meet him in Chapter Seven.

WHERE DO I MEET MR. RIGHT?

I can remember a time when I had this same question…well, similar….you know what I mean! I soon realized the answer to this question. Anywhere and everywhere! What? Too vague? Okay, I suppose that answer doesn't really help you out too much, so let's go into more detail. Just about every single one of the places below have produced dozens or even hundreds of dates for me over the years.

Online

If you are not already online, then where have you been? Anyone serious about finding someone should be online. It really doesn't have the same stigma that it used to, so if you are worried about what your friends might think then you are probably worrying unnecessarily. Some good sites are match.com, lavalife.com, pof.com and okcupid.com.

Men are going to look at your picture first. What you have written in your profile is secondary. If you are naturally gorgeous then most men will message you on that alone. But that doesn't mean you should be skimping on the profile. If you want to make it easier for him to message you something other than 'How are you?' then give him something that will make him want to get to know you better. Something he can refer to in his message. If your profile just says something like, 'ummmmm.... any questions you have, just ask!" Well, you are not telling him anything about yourself, so why is he going to message you other than the fact that he thinks you are hot? He doesn't know you from a hole in the wall. I have skipped over profiles of hot women before for that reason. Help him out. Make sure your profile is interesting. If you don't think you are as attractive as some of the other women out there (and you are, believe me. Everyone is beautiful in their own way) then you are going to have to sell him in the profile. He is there because he liked your pictures. Now you have to sell him on who you are and why you would be a match. Think, and be creative!

Have multiple pictures. The more the better. This way he will have a good idea as to what you really look like. Don't put up that one great pic where the light is hitting you just right. The pic may look great, but if it isn't a good depiction of what you really look like, then you are setting yourself up for disappointment.

Online dating can be like shopping at Marshalls. You have to go through racks and racks of crappy clothes just to find that one nice, designer item that fits you perfectly! Online dating takes patience, but it can be worth it.

I'll be talking about online dating in detail in the bonus chapter at the end of this book

Bars / clubs

This seems like an obvious choice for most singles, but this isn't really the best place to be meeting people for a serious relationship. It is not the real world at all, as neither men nor women are themselves in this environment. Bars and clubs are often loud and in some cases too loud to talk. How can you get to know someone when you are screaming in each others ears only to hear half of what the other person has to say? Is it possible to find Mr. Right in a bar? Anything is possible, but you will have to weed through a lot of bad apples before you get to the one truffle. Don't be afraid to be a little more challenging in these situations, but make sure you have fun with it. No need to be rude or bitchy, just be firm. Be who you are and have fun. Most importantly, don't take anything that happens in a bar too seriously. It isn't the real world remember! If a guy says something mean to you, then look for the humor in it and laugh! His rude comment was honestly more to protect his own fragile little ego than it is about you. After all, he doesn't even know you so why are you going to let it bother you?

Coffee shops

If you are at a coffee shop sitting down with a friend, then you may find it challenging getting a guy to come over to talk to you. It is always a lot harder when there is an audience, not to mention that he has to engage and captivate both of you and there is a much stronger chance of rejection. If you are alone however, it makes it much easier for him. Rather than just sitting there like a door knob, bring your laptop and do some work. At least make it look like you are working! If you see a guy you like, don't look too busy. Give him a quick glance. Be flirty and try to get him to come over. If you want to help him out further you could always just ask him what he is drinking and take it from there. Maybe he will take it further, maybe he won't, but it doesn't hurt to ask.

On the street

I'm not talking about standing on the street corner in mid-town Manhattan at 1 AM, but walking down the busy street in a populated downtown neighborhood. The key is that it needs to be busy as the odds you are going to encounter Mr. Right walking along a cul-de-sac in suburbia is pretty much non-existent. Make sure you aren't walking too quickly as if it looks like you are in a rush, he won't stop you. If you have a dog, all that much better as it gives him a reason to stop.

Stopping people on the street can be pretty unnatural

and most guys don't even think it is possible. The seduction community for guys (read the book **'The Game'** by Neil Strauss) encourages this, so if a guy is SUPER smooth while stopping you on the street, you can be fairly certain he has done this before. He may do it all the time, and perhaps even many times that day. This doesn't mean you should discredit him, accuse him, or look down on him in any way. Just be aware and on your guard. This is my preferred way of meeting women and I have met some absolutely amazing women this way. This is how I met Kelly, so it is definitely possible to meet some great guys this way. Even if the guy who approaches you on the street has approached hundreds of women before you, it is possible that he was looking for *you* all that time. I did it to meet Kelly, and I found her.

Bookstores

Bookstores are great places to meet as you can often find singles in them. Many of them have a Starbucks right inside so you are getting a bookstore and a coffee shop all in one! If you are looking at a specific book that he may be interested in as well or has read then it makes it easier for him to open you naturally. You can also open him if you see him looking at a book you have read. These situations allow for easy initial conversation that establishes a sincere commonality before any attraction is even developed.

Grocery stores

The one place where every single person ends up at one point or another, after all, they have to eat, right? After work is always a good time to go as many people are picking up groceries on the way home. There are a zillion things that a guy can talk to you about in a grocery store, or vice versa. “Why are they always out of the items on special?” “What the hell is a kumquat and how do you eat them?” Look at the items in their cart and say, “well aren’t you a healthy eater! You can actually turn that stuff into something that tastes good?” The options are endless.

Shopping malls

Walking through the halls of the mall is pretty much identical to meeting men on the street. Don’t be afraid to give a guy a little glance as you walk past to try to trigger him to approach. Just like on the street, I wouldn’t expect to get approached too often in these situations, as most guys don’t think it is even possible to approach this way. It is not as though they are puss-bags, it is just that running back to talk to someone is not everyday, socially accepted behavior, so it is very difficult for most men (I’ll be talking more about this later). The malls do have stores however, which they may find approaching you a little easier, just as in a grocery store.

Gym

Most people are busy working out, but if they are just casually walking on a treadmill, bike, or elliptical, then it doesn’t hurt to grab the one beside them and give them a quick, friendly smile. If you see someone working out on any of the machines or free weight stations then you can ask if you can work in with them. This gives great opportunity for conversation to start.

Airport

One of my favorite places to meet people! Are you flying away on business or for vacation and have a few hours to kill? Why not stroll around and see if Mr. Right might be sitting alone waiting for his business flight to board? It doesn't matter if you are on his flight or not, it doesn't hurt to sit beside him and ask him where he is going. Airports are probably the easiest way to start conversation, as the common element is travel. From there you can start talking about other places he has traveled to, if he travels for work and how often he travels. If he is at your own gate and on your flight, all that much better!

Seminars / Workshops

Seminars can have dozens, hundreds or even thousands of like-minded people at them. Many of them are set up in a way where you can easily network which makes it extremely easy to approach or get approached. Be talkative and fun and discuss your experiences about the seminar, what you have learned and what brought you there in the first place. That of course leads to additional discussion about other topics. A great one to check out that I think everyone should go to is the Millionaire Mind Intensive. www.millionairemindsecrets.info

Work

Not necessarily the greatest place to meet someone, especially if you see them every day, but people meet in the workplace all the time. If you work for a large enough company and the potential Mr. Right works in another department where you rarely see him, then why not. If he is in the cubicle right beside you, then not necessarily the best of ideas unless you can build a solid connection with him before any dating even begins. Then you have a shot, but just make sure to check with management on this. If not, prepare to do a lot of sneaking around, as that can be fun too!

Parties

This almost goes without saying, but definitely worth mentioning. Where else can you get warm introductions from your friends? If you don't know too many people at the party, it is very easy and perfectly acceptable to start by asking, "how do you know so-and-so?" People are typically very friendly at parties so a great way to meet people when they are in a social mood and often at their best. They will all be open to meeting you, so don't hold back regardless of what the outcome is. They won't assume you are hitting on them, they will assume you are just being social.

Sports leagues

Join a baseball, soccer, hockey, or volleyball league. It doesn't matter what the league is, it could be pea-shooting if that is what floats your boat. Just make sure it is co-ed and you have some kind of interest in playing. These types of environments give you lots of opportunity to meet people easily and in a non-threatening way.

Book clubs

Enjoy reading? You won't have any shortage of things to talk about with men you meet at a book club. If books are your thing then take a look and see if there is a book club in your area where you can meet other dorky people like yourself (totally kidding).

Singles parties

Try a Google search to see if there are any organized singles events in your area or try looking on meetup.com where you are almost guaranteed to find them. Need I say more?

Driving

Okay, so maybe this isn't the best one on the list. Actually, I don't really think this is a good one at all. In fact, it is horrible, but just thought I would throw it in here as I have secured dates while driving. The odds of you pulling up to a red light with Mr. Right in the car beside you with the windows down and starting up a striking conversation is pretty slim, but it does happen. He will almost definitely require some obvious flirty behavior on your part if you expect anything to start.

Lastly… If you are truly committed to meeting someone then you need to get out of the house! You aren't going to meet anyone sitting at home wondering why you are still single. Even if you have nowhere to go, head down to a local bar and chat up the bartender for entertainment and to practice your conversational skills. Go for a walk, or go shopping. Do you really need me to give you a reason to go shopping?

Chapter Three Highlights

- ✓ It is impossible to 'just know' if someone is the right person for you soon after meeting them. People are not really themselves in the early stages.
- ✓ You are in control of your life. Not your family or society. Do what YOU want to do.
- ✓ Identify exactly what you want in a man in every detail.
- ✓ Identify what you are attracted to, and then compare the two lists. This will ensure that what you want and what you are attracted to are in alignment.
- ✓ Know your deal breakers and honor them. No exceptions.
- ✓ You can meet Mr. Right anywhere and everywhere!
- ✓ Get out of the house!

You should now have a clear understanding of what you are looking for in Mr. Right and where to find him. Now it's time to look at how can you avoid wasting time with Mr. Wrong.

CHAPTER FOUR

MR. WRONG

"You build on failure. You use it as a stepping stone. Close the door on the past. You don't try to forget the mistakes, but you don't dwell on it. You don't let it have any of your energy, or any of your time, or any of your space."
~Johnny Cash

You should now have a good understanding of exactly what you are looking for and are much better positioned to recognize Mr. Right when you meet him. Now let's take a look at how you can identify Mr. Wrong, which is just as important. After all, if you are wasting time with Mr. Wrong, then you are shutting out the guy you truly want and deserve to be with, and that isn't fair to either of you.

If you are wasting time with Mr. Wrong, then you are shutting out the guy you truly want and deserve to be with.

Tom and Marie have been dating for almost two years. She is absolutely crazy about him, but he more or less keeps to himself. He never tells her he loves her (because he doesn't) and will only make time for her when it is convenient for him. Tom has never once referred to Marie as his girlfriend, nor does he plan to. In social situations, she gets introduced simply as 'Marie.' Tom makes a point to see Marie about once per week, and makes every effort to avoid seeing her anymore than that. That is all part of his plan. She may get the odd call or text from him, but these don't come too frequently. If she texts him, she may or may not get a response. Marie is faithful to Tom as she sees him as her boyfriend. Tom on the other hand is not faithful. He doesn't feel he has anyone to be faithful to, as to him, Marie is just a friend with benefits. She is convinced that deep down he will change and will start to love her. She knows that if she keeps trying, she will eventually win him over at which time they can have beautiful little kidlets and live happily ever after. Not going to happen.

Tom is flat out wasting Marie's time and she is allowing it to happen by hanging on to her wishful thinking. In this case, Tom is not respecting Marie and Marie is not respecting herself. She is living in la la land.

Don't become a Marie!

Many women are with the wrong guy, yet they continue to hang on thinking that things will change, or more specifically that he will change. I'll be talking more about changing him later. With many of my past relationships, the wrong guy was me, yet women would hang on, and so would I, for as long as I wanted to before I felt it was time to let them go. I have now moved on from that lifestyle, but I don't regret any of it as it helped make me the person I am today. I can now use that knowledge to help you identify when you may be wasting time chasing that one guy who you really don't have a shot with because he just doesn't care about you, nor will he ever. He knows it isn't going to work out. He knew that right from the beginning, yet he continues to give you false hope just because you stand there and let him. Well, we are going to put a stop to that right now.

BAITING THE CHASE

When someone you like is pushing you away and giving you reasons or clues that he is not interested in you, it is either because he is playing a game with you or just flat out not into you. What a lot of women do is start to chase, and men love it when they have women chasing them. Pick up artists and players have learned this to be a very effective tactic. They have learned to influence women's emotions in a way that will get them to chase. This is what makes some of them so successful with women. It is important for women to understand their emotions and not let them steer them down the wrong path, no matter how tempting it may be.

Both women, and men for that matter, may respond in a very needy way when they are pushed away. Some women will cling and do everything they can to try to 'win over' the guy. They do the things that would completely turn them off if the roles were reversed. While this may eventually result in seemingly 'getting' the guy… it does not set the grounds for a healthy relationship. In many cases, she is just setting herself up for disappointment. You are making it very easy for him to do whatever he wants with you and very often that will be having sex just for the sport of it. He doesn't give a crap who you really are as a person or how good you may be. Don't put yourself in this situation, as it is super needy.

It is important to give him reasons why you are a catch without coming across as needy. If he truly is a man of quality, he will ask you out and he will pursue. You may love to chase as many women do, but is chasing a guy that is not into you really going to get you what you want? Do you really want this guy or are you just getting caught up in the game and trying to avoid rejection? By giving him some space and not pursuing him like this, you can think a little clearer and make a more accurate decision as to whether this guy is right for you. Both men and women do this, so it is important to realize that there is balance. By pushing too hard, you may end up in a relationship with someone who has not thought it through. Pushing someone into a relationship is a recipe for disaster. There are lots of great guys out there that you will be equally as attracted to that want the same things you do.

CAN YOU CHANGE HIM?

Bill is one of the nicest guys you could possibly meet. He's caring, considerate, loves to help people and would never even consider doing anything to hurt someone. He has been dating Sandra for about a year, but he was never really that into her. He told her flat out, right from the beginning that he wasn't looking for anything serious with her even though she was looking for something serious with him. He reminded her of this frequently, yet she would often act as if they were married. In the end, she was disappointed when things didn't work out as she thought she could change him.

If you are in a situation where you are dating someone and he just doesn't seem to care, then he probably doesn't and you are wasting your time. Be very conscious of this as it happens far too frequently. You really have to ask yourself in these cases if he really does like you. He may like you… as a friend with benefits. Someone who can give him a release when he needs it. If that's what you are looking for then great, but don't think you are going to change him if this is all that you are to him. He likes you, but not in the way you want him to. In some cases, he may not even be that attracted to you, but attracted just enough for sexual flings. Many guys will lower their standards for women they are just interested in having sex with and nothing more. He won't tell you he isn't that attracted to you, nor will he even hint at it in any way. You simply don't know, regardless of how hot you think you may be.

If you are in a situation where you are dating someone and he just doesn't seem to care, then he probably doesn't and you are wasting your time.

WHAT ELSE ARE YOU MISSING OUT ON?

I was walking through the mall several years ago when I saw a beautiful woman standing by the water fountain that I just had to go talk to. She was a nice, shy girl, who turned out to be a lot of fun once she opened up. Natalie and I ended up dating for the next three years. It started off pretty casual and stayed casual most of the time despite her wanting more. While we had a lot of fun together, I always knew deep down that she wasn't really the right girl for me. We just seemed to be too different from one another, but she was great in so many ways. It took me about two and a half years before I finally called her my girlfriend, and about six months after that, she broke up with me. "You deserve to find someone who you can love as much as I love you," she told me. Good for her. That took a tremendous amount of courage to come forward with that. I have a large amount of respect for her, as I am sure that was not easy for her in the least. While I did love Natalie, I was never actually IN love with her, despite her being such a great girl.

So how much more time are you going to waste by dating the wrong guy? Don't you think you could quite possibly be missing out on something better?

If you think you may be dating the wrong guy now then you are probably right. If you find that you are continually dating the wrong guy then your thinking patterns need to change. The crucially important exercises I outlined in Chapter Three will help you identify your negative patterns to put you on track to change the type of guys you usually end up with. Make a conscious effort to stay connected with this way of thinking. By wasting time with the wrong guy, you are completely ripping off your

Mr. Right who is out there right now looking for YOU, not to mention ripping yourself off at the same time.

By wasting time with the wrong guy, you are completely ripping off your Mr. Right, who is out there right now looking for YOU.

THE SECOND RATE RELATIONSHIP

Sometimes people know they are not right for each other, but stay together anyway just because it is comfortable or that they don't want to break up with the other person for fear of hurting them. Sometimes, staying together just seems easier. But if you are unhappy in the relationship and he is not, then isn't that one sided? Isn't a relationship supposed to be a partnership? By staying together just because you think it is easier, you are being nothing short of selfish. Is that who you really are? I doubt it.

You may be afraid of hurting him, but these cases typically end up with someone being hurt anyway. The outcome is often worse than it would have been if you were up front in the beginning. If a couple is together who aren't right for each other, they will still develop feelings, but they are never as strong as what they could be. By hanging in there, you are depriving yourself of feelings that could be far more powerful. Don't let his feelings develop if you are not into him. Don't let your own mediocre feelings develop for him as you just make the situation all that much more confusing and difficult for yourself. You know what is best and you know what you have to do, so stop over thinking it. Give him the boot and move on to what you really want. You owe it to yourself to find the guy you deserve to be with. Don't settle for a second rate relationship.

You owe it to yourself to find the guy you deserve to be with.

EX-BOYFRIENDS

Natalie and I ended up staying in touch for the next couple of years, although our relationship was purely platonic at that point. As much as I wanted to jump her, I just couldn't do that because of how much respect I had for her. I didn't want to hurt her anymore than I already had. Finally, she told me she needed to move on and was making some changes in her life. She said she didn't think it was a good idea for us to continue to stay in touch. Once again, I applaud her. By staying in touch with your ex, ESPECIALLY the one you have feelings for, you are always going to have that person in the back of your mind. Until you cut them loose completely, it will be all that much more difficult for you to move on to find the right person. You may think deep down that there is a chance the two of you will still get together, when he probably knows that will never happen. Don't waste time like this. By staying in touch with your past boyfriends, you are sabotaging your future. There isn't a single one of my ex-girlfriends that I stay in touch with today. I stay in touch with several women

I have had more casual relationships with, but not a single one where we were involved in anything serious.

This applies to guys you like that you aren't getting anywhere with as well. By moving on you will significantly increase your chances of finding the right person. It is really hard to move forward with these people in your life. To paraphrase the old adage, 'if you love someone then set him free, if he comes back to you then it is meant to be.'

By staying in touch with your past boyfriends, you are sabotaging your future.

Chapter Four Highlights

- ✓ Don't waste time with the wrong guy.
- ✓ Don't chase a man who starts to pull back. When you chase it makes it very easy for him to have sex with you just for the sport of it.
- ✓ Chasing can come across as needy.
- ✓ If a guy says he doesn't want a relationship or anything serious, don't think you can change him.
- ✓ If he doesn't seem to care, then he doesn't. He is wasting your time.
- ✓ If you think you may be dating the wrong guy, then you probably are.
- ✓ By wasting time with the wrong guy, you are completely ripping off Mr. Right, who is out there looking for you.

Not to mention, you are ripping yourself off at the same time.

- ✓ Don't stay in a relationship just because it feels 'comfortable' or 'okay'. Don't settle for a second rate relationship!
- ✓ Cut ex-boyfriends out of your life.
- ✓ Dump anyone you are dating who you aren't getting anywhere with.

Now it's time to look at your perception of the men who approach you as well as their perception of you.

CHAPTER FIVE

REALITY, WHAT IS REAL?

"To effectively communicate, we must realize that we are all different in the way we perceive the world and use this understanding as a guide to our communication with others."
~Tony Robbins

Sometimes women get approached by men a lot, particularly out at a bar or club where it is the norm to approach strangers. The hotter men perceive the girl to be, the more she will tend to get approached. For many women, this can get flat out annoying, especially when it seems like the guys they aren't interested in are always the ones that end up approaching. These guys may all say the exact same thing too. "How are you, what do you do, where are you from?" Doesn't it get a little stale? Of course it does. If you have ten different guys approach you in an evening all saying the exact same thing then it is only natural to become a little standoffish. These women have to throw up some kind of shield to protect them from the barrage of bore they are bombarded with. This can often make them come across as 'bitches' when really they are far from it in the 'real world', and clubs are not the 'real world'.

It was 2:10am on a Friday and Mary and Jane had just left a night club. They decided to get a bite to eat at the hot dog cart around the corner. They were dressed to the nines and looked fantastic. Tony and Kyle were hungry and were thinking about grabbing a dog as well. As soon as Tony got in line behind the two girls, Jane spun around and spoke quite sternly "Don't even THINK about talking to us!"

What a bitch! The guys thought. This was an unnecessary and extreme reaction to a situation that had not even happened yet. The girls' reaction was out of pure frustration from the probably dozens of times they had been approached with the same boring stuff that evening. They clearly had enough of it and didn't want to have to deal with one more 'loser'. While they most likely picked up on some subtle body language from Tony (after all, he WAS going to try to talk to her), being flat out rude wasn't necessary either. It's a negative energy that doesn't help anyone.

This 'protection shield' that many women throw up can help to weed out the weaker men. This is why it needs to be there in some situations where they are approached frequently, but it can be done in a fun and challenging way. It doesn't have to be rude. It takes a lot of courage for men to approach as many of them have a strong fear of getting a reaction similar to what Jane gave Tony. Jane really doesn't have to give Tony the time of day if she doesn't want to, nor does she need to talk to him at all. Just turning her back on him after a subtle acknowledgment would be sufficient nine times out of ten. If the guy continues to persist, then by all means, be progressively firmer with him until he gets the hint. Some guys will continue pushing until you make it very clear that his presence is unwelcome. Don't be afraid to be a little firmer when need be or you may have Danny Douchebag clinging off of you all night, but just try not to be rude initially.

MAKING ASSUMPTIONS

While some women who get approached a lot can often be construed as 'bitchy' at first, this of course isn't who they really are. In fact, many of them are some of the most caring and sweetest people I have ever met. They just put on that 'front' to protect themselves from the multitudes of seemingly unsuitable men that approach them continually. If this 'front' you are putting on is not really who you are, then what makes you so certain their approach style is really who they are? We need to determine what is real and what isn't as it can be very easy to make assumptions.

When people first meet, they don't yet know each other, so they will naturally make certain assumptions about the other person. They can't spend the time or energy required to find out more about what their deal really is, so they go with their gut. They make assumptions based on what the person says, their body language, how they react and how they look. This is more commonly referred to as judging. Judging definitely has a negative connotation to it, but that is essentially what you are doing when you make assumptions. In this particular case, there is nothing wrong with that. Women are excellent readers of body language and if a man has unattractive body language, he won't stand a chance with her regardless of what he is saying or how he looks. They are making an assumption based on his body language.

PERCEPTION IS REALITY

Your perception of any given situation is reality in your mind. If you believe something to be real, then you accept it as real, regardless of whether it is true or false, good or bad. This is a very powerful concept. You can attach whatever meaning you like to any given situation. You choose what things mean to you. It is you that define the outside circumstances, and not the outside circumstances that define you. Often the meaning you attach to a situation is wrong! If you are going to be wrong anyway, then why not attach a meaning that is going to support you and your goals? What you are doing here is forming opinions in your mind and then accepting them as facts.

If you believe something to be real, then you accept it as real, regardless of whether it is true or false, good or bad.

This can be quite frustrating for a guy who likes you and knows that you two would get along great. However you have attached a false meaning to something and accepted it as reality, which is now going to prevent any sort of relationship from ever getting started. These situations are a shame as there is so much happiness that is falling through the cracks for both people. I am not saying that you are never right, but be conscious that your perception of the situation may not be reality. This happens all the time when men and women first meet. Be on guard about initial 'perceptions' about a guy. Often they are incorrect. Always look at several possible meanings and then choose the one that supports you. If it turns out that the negative meaning was the correct one, you will find out soon enough anyway. Make sure you give yourself that extra chance for success.

HOW INTERESTING ARE YOU?

More common than a woman coming across as bitchy, she may often come across as boring or uninteresting. In some cases this is conscious behavior on her part, but in others it may be because she is nervous or shy. While she may like the guy, it doesn't come across that way. This is the same nervousness that can seriously affect a man's performance when he approaches you. To a lot of men, casually strolling up to a woman and starting a conversation, be it in a bar or in another environment can be quite scary. Even if it is something he does all the time, the fear will still be there. However, he has learned how to handle himself better in these situations. A good thing? Yes and no. This could mean he is a player, or it could be that he is just committed to finding his future wife, but don't assume one way or another. Just as you may not be yourself due to nervousness when you're approached by a guy you like, he may not be either. The more attraction one has for the other, the harder it will be for both of them to focus. I'll be going over this in more detail in Chapter Ten. The next time a guy approaches you, be conscious of this before you discredit him TOO quickly. You will still be eliminating many of the men who approach you, don't get me wrong, but if you are going to discredit him, make sure you do it for the right reasons.

THE HIDDEN MEANING

Women can have a tendency to search and hunt for the hidden meaning in everything. While there are many cases where there is one, there are also many cases where there isn't. Often the clues you need are right in front of you. As a woman, you are naturally gifted for picking up on a lot of little things that men would miss. There is a lot to be said for women's intuition, but always be conscious as to whether you are overanalyzing a situation. Make sure you have enough evidence before forming a conclusion. Very often, there is no hidden meaning at all. There are always going to be instances where the guy screws up and says something stupid. Especially if he really likes you and is a little more on the nervous side BECAUSE he doesn't want to screw up. In many cases it can be a trivial detail.

When a man messes up, understand that he is human and don't make assumptions that discredit him immediately. This of course depends on the severity of his screw up, but if you otherwise had a great time with him, you may want to give him more of a chance before kicking him to the curb. If you were having a good time with him to this point, you will probably continue having a good time with him as you get to know him better. Don't let something stupid end the interaction, especially something that you may be misinterpreting entirely, or taking out of context.

Sometimes a guy may come off as arrogant, or trying to impress, but in many cases he is just trying to make a good impression or show that he is confident in himself. Is he really that arrogant? There is no question that some guys are arrogant pricks, but don't assume that right away, take the time to find out for sure. I've been called arrogant many times! I don't think I am at all. I may be a little cocky sometimes, but I do it in a way that makes ME laugh and puts me in a better mood. I will also frequently engage in self-deprecating humor, as that also makes me laugh. Does that mean I really feel that way about myself? Absolutely not! But it's pretty funny sometimes!

Just as a guy can come across as arrogant, a woman may come across as being a bitch, but in most cases, she really isn't at all. She just may be shy and nervous, because SHE wants to make a good impression, just as the guy does. You see how I put a positive spin on it? Whether she is or isn't doesn't matter to me at this point. Until I have a bit more information, I'll continue to view her in a positive light.

Chapter Five Highlights

- ✓ You don't know a person when you first meet them, so be conscious of any assumptions you make.
- ✓ Perception is reality. If you believe something is real, you accept it as reality regardless of how wrong you may be.
- ✓ Don't form opinions and then accept them as facts until you have more evidence.

- ✓ You can attach whatever meaning you like to any situation. Come up with multiple meanings and go with the one that best serves you.
- ✓ Be weary of always trying to find the hidden meaning in everything. Often there isn't one.

CHAPTER SIX

THE GAME

"The game has its ups and downs, but you can never lose focus of your individual goals and you can't let yourself be beat because of lack of effort."
~Michael Jordan

You will often hear both men and women talking about how they hate to play games. 'Why can't people just be honest with each other? Why can't people just be themselves?' Let me ask you this.... Would you like to be swept off your feet by Mr. Right? Or do you want some dude to walk up to you awkwardly saying that you are really hot and that he would like to go out on a date with you, without building any attraction or value whatsoever? Would you like a guy to call you five times per day to tell you how much he likes you and that he can't wait to see you again after only talking to you for five minutes? Or would you prefer someone who has a more relaxed attitude? How about so much of a relaxed attitude that he shows no interest in you at all? If a guy shows what you perceive to be too much interest, as a result you discredit him. If he shows just a little interest, then you start to become intrigued. If you like him and he doesn't respond at all then it may even drive you crazy.

If a guy really likes you, he will want to show interest, but he knows too much too soon will drive you away. He has to hold back a little bit if he wants to have a shot with you. This alone could be considered game playing as he is altering his behavior in order to boost his chances of success with you. Many women say they don't want players, but end up rejecting a perfectly good mate solely because he doesn't play the game. This is the game on its most basic level, and of course it gets far more advanced than this, but this is where it starts.

So is this manipulation or is this just human psychology?

'The Game' really does have a negative connotation to it, but really it is just an unofficial nickname for 'human psychology.' In an ideal world, you would find Mr. Right without having to put in any effort. You would become rich without having to work for it, and all war and crimes would come to an end, but unfortunately, that isn't the world we live in, so action needs to be taken if you truly want to get what you want. It isn't perfect, but it is what it is and all we can do is make the best out of it.

I don't like the term 'playing games.' After all, we aren't playing games, we are looking at getting you together with Mr. Right as serious business. It is not about manipulating people, it is about understanding and leveraging psychology to build attraction with the opposite sex. Manipulation implies you are lying and deceiving in order to trick someone into giving you something for your sole benefit. That isn't what you are trying to do at all! You are trying to build value and create attraction from men, and you don't need to lie or be dishonest to do it.

ARE *YOU* A PLAYER?

You have been playing the game in the past whether you realize it or not. Since you have been doing it anyway, you may as well be conscious of it so you can use it to your advantage with the guys that you really want.

Sometimes you may engage in playing when you are not sure how much you like a guy. You don't care whether you see him or not, you could take it or leave it. But when he pushes the right buttons, you start to really like him. All of a sudden you do care. Your 'game playing' kept him interested in you and he followed through eventually winning you over. You fall in love, get married, have kids, and grow old together. The end. Was there a loser in that situation? Absolutely not!

Remove the negative connotation on game playing and just call it building attraction with someone who intrigues you. You want to show them you are different from all the other women, so make sure you keep his interest. If you come too easy for him, he won't value you anywhere near as much as he would if he had to work to make your relationship happen. Have fun with it because it really is a fun process when you do it correctly and it works out for everyone in the end. It is a win-win situation, so don't deprive him of it and more importantly, don't deprive yourself of it. Trust me, people want to play a little. They just don't realize it and that goes for men and women alike. It keeps the interaction interesting to both sides and improves chances of success.

People want to be challenged in life, and I am not just talking about dating. When you face more challenging situations, you sharpen your skills and become more aware. It keeps you moving forward in life. The bigger the challenge, the better you feel when you overcome it. Do accomplishments mean more to you when they come without any effort at all or when they were a challenge for you to achieve? These same principals can apply equally as well to dating. Even if someone just likes you a bit, they will like you a lot more if they have to work a little to get you. Catch my drift? It's not at all about manipulation. Just make sure you aren't lying or doing anything deceptive and everyone is happy in the end. Most importantly, have fun with it!

**Even if someone just likes you a bit,
they will like you a lot more if
they have to work a little to get you.**

ATTRACTION

Attraction is something that isn't always there at first and sometimes it needs to be created. You will sometimes see an attractive girl with a far less attractive guy and you often may wonder why she would be with a guy like that. Well, most guys wonder that all the time when we see this. I'd be willing to bet that the girl didn't just see the guy and become instantly attracted to him. He had to build it with her. So what makes people attracted to each other? They can be different things for both men and women. Men are more attracted to the physical while women's attraction is more emotional. Men are focusing more on what you look like where as women are focusing on the way the man makes them feel. This is the way it is at first at least. It is going to take a lot more than your looks to land Mr. Right permanently, but you must attract him first.

Attraction works at different speeds with men and women. Women can be compared with an electric stove. They take a while to heat up. Men can be more compared with a gas fireplace where it heats up at the flick of a switch. So what exactly attracts men and women to one another?

Women are attracted to:

- Intelligence
- Sense of Humor / Personality
- Confidence
- Men who are challenging
- Leadership among friends
- Power/Status (leadership, fame)
- Social intuition. Is he awkward around other people or your friends?
- How well does he fit in?
- Pre-selection by women (more on this later)

- Looks (particularly height)
- Dress
- Means/wealth

Men are attracted to:

- Smile
- Hair
- Teeth
- Body type
- Eyes
- Dress
- Sense of Humor / Personality
- Intelligence

Notice how the men's list is primarily looks driven? Now, once he meets you and is attracted he is going to want to see that you have personality and a brain. But that won't be what initially attracts him.

Now you may be thinking, but Paul, women are attracted to all those things on the men's list as well. Yes, I am very aware of that, however a man can build attraction with a woman without the physical features being present, where it would be very difficult for a woman to do the same with a man. We are just too visual. It's not the way it SHOULD be, but it is the way it IS. You may think this is shallow, but let me ask you this. Have you ever rejected a man because he is too short or because he has a receding hairline? So what is the difference? It is imperative that you are physically attracted, and this goes for both men and women. It is not about being shallow.

Just as women are attracted to all the things on the men's list as well, men can be attracted to much of what is on the woman's list, but it is always going to be looks driven first and everything else afterward.

The more physically attractive the woman is, the more frustrated with men she may tend to get. Even the most solid men can become weak at the knees around a stunningly attractive woman (regardless of how they may seem to come across on the outside). A guy may be more fearful making moves, which can often cause him to screw it up for himself (and for her for that matter). If a man is hesitant to move in for a kiss when the time is right, she may start to lose attraction for him all together. She wants him to be able to take charge and lead the emotional progression. If he fails to do this, she may completely lose attraction for him all together.

When a man approaches you, the first thing he tries to do is build his value in order get you interested. Sometimes he doesn't build any value at all and will just right away ask you for your number, particularly if he is not that skilled with women. There are many women who will give their number in this case even though he hasn't really built any real value for himself. It is crucial that the man builds value as you don't want to give your number to just anyone. You probably aren't going to take his call or return his texts in this case anyway, so why bother. Not to mention, you're creating a false hope for him as well.

Once he builds value and you like him you will then naturally start to build your value to him. He should be legitimately interested in you for more than just your looks at this point, and he very well may be trying to pretend to be if you are more attractive. The more attractive you are, the more that may be the case and therefore the slower you need to proceed. Tread lightly, but don't be too critical at the same time. How do you know he is being sincere? You will need to test him for congruency.

CONGRUENCY TESTS

As I stated in the section on body language back in chapter two, women can be more perceptive than men and can pick up on inconsistencies in body language. In these cases, it is always the body language that the woman perceives as being correct. In fact, if she detects these inconsistencies, she may not listen to him at all. What she is picking up on is incongruence. Words should match the body language. You may have to throw him some curves in order to 'test' to ensure he stays congruent. You may even be doing this now but not realizing you are doing it. In some cases, the woman can come across as being bitchy, particularly if she is being approached by lots of men. It can no doubt get frustrating at times which can force them to test.

You want to be careful you aren't overly challenging in these cases. It is a fine line. Start off small and work your way up and gauge his reactions. Congruency tests don't all have to done at the first meeting. They can be done on the first date as well or even beyond. If you like him, give him a bit of a chance before testing and be careful you don't accidentally send the wrong signals causing him to lose interest. A pick up artist or player will continue to put up with all the BS (if it turns from a simple congruency test to

BS) and may continue pushing through, but I assure you any regular and decent man isn't going to put up with it, so be careful. It can be very easy for her to screw things up for herself (and for him) by being purposely uninteresting, unresponsive, bitchy or overly challenging. Again, if you like him, test by all means, but tread lightly while doing so.

All you are really going to do to test for congruency is to challenge him on things he says. You want to find out if it is true or if it is BS. For example, if he says he is an astronaut, you could come right back and say "You're not an astronaut!" Then see how he qualifies himself to you. He may get defensive, he may try to overly qualify himself to you, or he may respond in a calm and cool manner and not really care what you think. If he gives you either of the first two responses, and he will no doubt lose value. After all, shouldn't an astronaut be able to handle such a simple challenge? Anything else would be incongruent.

People don't place as much value on anything that comes easily, so put up a bit of a challenge and he will value you all that much more. Just be careful not to go overboard with it. I can't say enough that being overly challenging will only end up driving good men away and you may be left dating players or pick up artists.

If you dangle a string just out of a cats reach, the cat will go crazy trying to get the string. You could have him doing back flips, front flips, side flips (if such a thing exists, I am sure you could get the cat to do it!) and just about anything to get that string. But what happens as soon as you drop the string down in front of the cat, handing it to Fluffy on a silver platter? Fluffy loses complete interest in it. The same applies to human psychology as well. Keep him at arms length during the early stages of the relationship and you will drive him crazy (in a good way!). Don't be too available, don't always return his calls or texts right away, and don't be afraid to end phone conversations first (more on this later). By keeping the string just out of his reach, spending time with you is going to be all that much more precious to him.

MEN WHO ARE 'PRE-SELECTED'

You may not have as much interest in a guy until you see him with other women. All of a sudden, he is desirable. For what reason? What did he just do that all of a sudden makes him the one for you? Don't worry if you can't come up with an answer for that one, as it is part of your programing. It is natural for women to be attracted to a man when they see he has already been pre-selected by other women. This is not just evident in the human world, but in the animal kingdom as well. The female sage grouse is much more likely to mate with a male who has just mated with another female. Also, if a stuffed female grouse is placed in the company of a male, that male becomes more attractive to them, which draw them over. Even in guppy fish, if a female guppy has a choice between two males, one of which is alone and the other is courting a female, the female will be attracted to the one doing the courting, regardless of whether the other female is still there.[1]

When women see other women surrounding a man, they start to wonder what he is all about and why he has all these women around him. If he is engaging all these

[1] Ridley, Matt (1993) The Red Queen- Sex and the Evolution of Human Nature. New York, NY HarperCollins Publishers Inc.

women, then there must be something he is doing right. Regardless of whether you are a man or a woman, we are always drawn to what we can't have. It is no different when we were children. There was always that toy that we didn't care to play with. That is, until it was taken away. We would then do whatever we need to in order to get the toy back. This is why some women are attracted to married men. They want what they can't have and it drives some women nuts to the point where this is who they start pursuing.

COMING ON TOO STRONG

Just as it is bad to be overly challenging, it is bad go in the other direction as well by coming on too strong. The more attracted you are and the more you like a guy, the more you will be tempted to break the 'rules' and engage in actions that are contradictory to getting you what you really want. The more you break these rules, the easier it is for the guy to prey on you and the harder you make it for yourself. The more you push, the more he will pull back. The more he pulls back, the harder you try and the harder you try, the more you lower your value. The end result is that you appear very needy. He knows he has you in the palm of his hand. You will NEVER turn a guy around after reaching this point. Men do this ALL the time with women and women do it with men and it works the same either way.

A few years ago, I was out at a lounge with my friend Mike where he introduced me to his friend Helen. She made it very clear that she liked me at that time, but I didn't show much interest in her. We ended up making out in my car later that evening and she was aggressively trying to pull me back to her place. I was going to go, but she had no available visitor parking and there was no other practical parking available, so we bailed on the idea. She texted me a bunch of times after that, but I was never very responsive as I wasn't that into her.

A few months later, Mike and I were going out again and he had asked Helen to come. She wasn't going to come out until she found out I was going to be there, at which point she said she would start getting ready right away. While we were in line to get into the lounge, Helen showed up and gave me a big hug. We started talking for a bit but I was engaged with my other friends as well, not to mention talking to other women in the line. A few minutes later she said, "I see you talking to other girls and I don't like it." I responded with, "well you better get used to it, because I am going to be talking to a lot more once we get inside." I'm not sure who she thought I was, or what obligation she thought I had to speak with her exclusively, but somehow she thought I would be fully engaged in her and her only. She then said, "Every girl I see you speaking with I am going to try to screw it up for you." I remember thinking, hmmmmm, this should be interesting and will almost definitely be fun. Let's see what happens!

Inside the bar, every time she saw me speaking with another girl, she would try to make out with me, therefore 'ruining' my chances with her. She would then go on to tell them she was my girlfriend. I was thinking to myself, "this is perfect! Helen is the best wing woman ever and she doesn't even realize it!" The women would then turn to me asking if this is true, at which point I would tell them the truth about me not even really knowing her and that she is a friend of a friend. I would instantly notice a spike in attraction from them. This is a perfect example of how pre-selection by women can be a major attraction switch. I knew I wasn't going to go home with Helen, that's for sure, but I did end up getting together with two of the many women I spoke to that evening.

DON'T be a Helen!

Don't come across as being needy by coming on too strong or it will never work out well for you in the end. It will kill any chance of a good relationship with anyone! Want to get rid of a guy? Be needy and that will do it pretty freaking quick. If the tables were turned and a man exhibited this sort of behavior toward you, you would be extremely turned off. Be conscious of that to ensure you don't make the same mistake. I'll bet you've met that one guy who seemed too easy for you. You didn't trust him then, and so you shouldn't have. If a guy expresses strong feelings too early, you'll doubt that those feelings are legitimate. You'll want to know that he will continue to feel that way should the relationship progress. If a man comes on too strong, there is a good chance you may lose attraction for him and you may doubt his intentions and his suitability as long term partner.

This is your 'women's intuition' at work and you need to trust it. It is like a sixth sense to you guys! The sooner he expresses interest without a compelling reason, the less attracted to him you may feel. This doesn't make sense to a lot of men, which is why many do not respect the space and the stages they need to go through in order to attract you. They forget about the attraction phase and try to move straight into comfort building. They tell you what they think you want to hear, instead of being genuine. This is not only insincere, but isn't going to get them anywhere either.

Men are nowhere near as complicated and we would react quite differently if the roles were reversed. If you exhibit this same sort of direct and complimentary behavior towards us, we won't lose attraction for you. You are however making it easy for us to take advantage of you, not to mention you are being just as insincere as 'that guy' described above. I could have easily done whatever I wanted to with Helen that evening, I just chose not to. There are many men however who would have seized the opportunity. You always have to pull back and get the guy to chase and never come on so strongly. Not only will this help you build true attraction and get the guys attention, but it also keeps you in the drivers seat and it won't be anywhere near as easy for him to take advantage of you.

VALIDATION

Do guys know what turns women off? In many cases they really have no clue. They may give you insincere compliments or just plain too many. They may flash money around thinking that is going to pique your interest. They may talk about themselves too much (more on this later) or may just come across as too cocky or arrogant. I already mentioned that men try to use logic for everything, so what seems logical when you like someone? Try to get their approval. A guy may agree with everything you say, laugh at your jokes (when they aren't funny), give you too many compliments, or put up with second rate behavior just to try to get you to like them. This approval seeking will seldom get you what you want.

What's ironic is this is exactly what many women will do with men when they really like someone. It isn't as much of a turn off for us as it is for you. At least not in the beginning. The more you seek our approval and look for validation, the easier it will be for men to play games with you. You are now an easy target. SOOO ridiculously easy I can't even put it into words. Just as guys should be conscious of this behavior, it is almost more important for a woman to be. I say this because if a guy acts that way, a woman may just give him the cold shoulder and he won't have a chance. However when a woman acts this way, she opens herself up to being taken advantage of, and quite easily at that.

The more you seek our approval and look for validation, the easier it will be for men to play games with you.

Not seeking approval can be difficult when you really like someone. The more you like someone, the harder you may try to get him to like you. As soon as he pulls away, you redouble your efforts. The chase begins. The more he pulls away, the more you chase. In a similar situation with the guy chasing you, you would naturally lose interest, as he would seem desperate. Don't make the same mistake. The more you like someone, the harder it can be, as you want to get their approval soooo badly, but don't sacrifice who you are to get it.

A man appreciates a woman with a mind of her own, just as you expect the guy to have one. Don't approval seek and don't chase. Speak your mind. If you don't like something or don't want to do something, then express that and don't pretend otherwise. This isn't a popularity contest, it is about trying to find the right person for you. If he doesn't like you for who you are then is he really the right person?

"I would rather be hated for who I am
than loved for who I am not."
~ Kurt Cobain

Love who you are and others will love you. Don't pretend to be who you are not.

Chapter Six Highlights

- ✓ Everyone hates playing games in relationships, but you have been playing them in the past whether you realize it or not. It isn't game playing, just human psychology.
- ✓ People want to play the game a little. They just don't realize it. Otherwise it would be far too easy. Playing the game is really nothing more than building attraction.
- ✓ Your looks are most important in building attraction, whether you look at that as shallow or not, that is the way it is. Accept it and do something about it.
- ✓ Once you have attracted him with your looks, you will

need to show that you have a personality as well. Looks will only take you so far.

- ✓ The more attractive you are, the slower you will need to go as you will want to be certain that he is interested in YOU and not just interested in your looks.
- ✓ Test a man for congruency to ensure he is being sincere.
- ✓ When you first meet a guy, it is okay to challenge, but don't be overly challenging. It is a fine line.
- ✓ Don't come on too strong! It makes it very easy for men to play with you.
- ✓ Never attach a single meaning to any one thing a guy says, either good or bad. Come up with multiple meanings and then ask yourself which one is most logical.
- ✓ Don't approval seek or chase in any way! It can come across as being super needy and makes you an easy target for men just looking for sex. A man appreciates a woman with a mind of her own.

"Hi I'm Bill." "Hi I'm Mary." Great, you have met! So now what?

CHAPTER SEVEN

MEETING

FACE TO FACE WITH MR. RIGHT

"You can make more friends in two months by becoming interested in other people than you can in two years by trying to get other people interested in you."
~Dale Carnegie

Jackie has been using online dating for a few months now without much success. That is, until she met Kyle, who appeared different from all the rest. Even after texting and talking on the phone for just a couple of weeks, Jackie could tell that he was a great guy. He would playfully tease her, and was always making her laugh. She loved it. She agreed to finally meet him the following weekend. A few days before the date, she was in a bookstore where she happened to pick up the book "The Game" by Neil Strauss. As she read through the book, she noticed that the guys in it would playfully tease women to get them laughing in order to build attraction. Jackie was shocked. This seemed to be exactly what Kyle was doing with her! Even though she was having a great time with him on the phone, she now assumed he was a player and canceled the date. She never returned another text or call from Kyle again.

So was Kyle a player? Jackie will unfortunately never find out as she labeled him and then accepted it as reality.

IS HE A LITTLE....*TOO* SMOOTH?

Are you waiting for the smooth guy? Some women may say they want a guy who will come and sweep them off their feet and then when he does, they reject him thinking he is a player. "He was too smooth, I don't trust him, he must be doing this all the time." Does that sound like the road to success with men to you?

If he is that smooth, then you are almost certainly right. If he seems to be saying all the right things and pushing all the right buttons, you can pretty much take to the bank that he has experience with women and has done this before, and most likely, many times before.

But does this mean you should be eliminating him as a possibility?

This is why it is so important to be clear on what you want. Don't jump to conclusions, as you need to find more evidence first. If he is in fact a player, you have to identify him as such first, before you make any harsh decisions. Maybe he is doing this all the time, but maybe he is doing it just to find you! These are the thoughts my girlfriend Kelly had about me when I originally approached her (she actually wrote that down in her notes while helping me edit this book). Sure, you can go ahead and assume he is a player (and you may be right), but don't label him without taking the time to find out for sure. Kelly took the time to find out, and I am more serious about her than any other girl I have ever met. The tools in this book will help you figure out if he is in fact the real deal or not. Men are really not that complicated and with a little bit of insight into the male mind, they can be pretty easy to figure out.

APPROACHING

Every interaction starts off before you meet. You see a guy that you really like, but you stand there and wait for him to make his move. You wait patiently, yet nothing happens. "I wish he would just come over and talk to me!" There are some women who think it is easy for men to approach women they are attracted to, but nothing could be further from the truth. Even the most seasoned pick up artist will still get anxiety before approaching a new girl, it is just that he has learned to act in spite of his fear.

Lets play a bit of a game here. Close your eyes and imagine this.... There is a guy that you would really like to go over and start talking to. You know there is no way he is going to come up and start talking to you first, and lets say in our little imaginary game, that there is little chance anyone else will either. (The vast majority of men do not have women walking up to them regularly regardless of who they are or what they look like). You decide that you are going to approach him, yet you keep thinking that there is a solid chance that you will get rejected. He could also quite possibly respond in a mean way, or you could end up looking foolish. In your mind, he is getting approached by women all the time. You walk up to meet him and what do you say? Think about that for a minute. You want to get his attention to see what he is all about. Can you think of anything creative? How does this pressure make you feel? Do you think you will be able to be your natural self when you are feeling this kind of anxiety? It isn't easy to just be yourself when you are feeling the pressure from social anxiety. Unless the guy is approaching women regularly and frequently, (and most good men aren't) this is what goes through his mind. In fact, most guys will probably not even bother approaching to begin with and the thing that stops them is the same thing that stops you from doing this in the first place. That thing is fear. Either fear of rejection, or fear of looking foolish. They may pace back and forth trying to think of the perfect thing to say, but they are lost. Their anxiety is running through the roof as they break into a cold sweat. They anticipate a negative reaction and then play this reaction over and over in their minds and then accept it as reality. The end result is that they don't approach.

GIVING SUBTLE HINTS

It is unlikely a guy is going to approach you out of the blue unless you give him some sort of signal. Guys are always looking for signals. Most guys want to approach you, but they need some sort of invitation. Some action is required on your part in order to give them a hint.

Nadia saw a guy she would just love to meet. He was about six feet tall, appeared to be fit, was dressed in an Armani suit and was very well groomed. From the outside, he appeared to be her dream man. She walked over to stand near him hoping he would approach her, but she kept her back to him, as she didn't want to seem obvious. He wasn't giving her the time of the day, so time for the next signal. A slight hair flip and an adjustment of her blouse. "He is sure to pick up on that and talk to me," she thought. No dice. Her dream man didn't notice her at all and ended up leaving without ever knowing she existed. While some of these 'clues' she was giving may have just been subconscious, it is very unlikely giving little signals like this are actually going to work.

It is not uncommon for women to give men a very subtle 'clue' that she is interested in him. Let me tell you something. The vast majority of guys will not pick up on subtle clues. Men are very often oblivious to subtle signals and they will go completely unnoticed ninety-nine percent of the time. He will most likely notice only if he is a seasoned pick up artist or player. We know these aren't the men you want, so in order to stop attracting them, you need to change a few things.

Men are quite dimwitted when it comes to picking up on signals. It may seem like you have to hit the guy over the head to get him to understand you are interested. I have met many women that would not even make eye contact with me only to find out later that they were interested.

Tiny signals like the ones mentioned above are not going to work. Medium sized signals aren't going to work either. Men need large, 'hit them over the head with a bat' type signals. If something seems like it would be too obvious, then you are probably on the right track. If you aren't sending out solid signals, then it is unlikely you will get approached by the guy you are interested in. Again, most men don't even think it is possible to approach a woman in common day to day life, so don't think they are going to do it without a solid signal. What would be a solid signal? Making strong eye contact and smiling, coyly looking away, then re-establishing eye contact is a solid signal. If he doesn't pick up on that, then he is either attached, lacks the confidence to approach, or is gay (or all three). In any of those cases, you don't want him anyway.

If you aren't sending out solid signals, then it is unlikely you will get approached by the guy you are interested in.

Don't worry about being too flirty or aggressive at this stage, as you are going to pull back once you have gotten his attention. Once you have his attention, you can sit back and let him do the chasing. But just because you have him physically attracted and talking to you doesn't mean your work is done. Now it is time to dazzle him with your superstar personality.

HAVE SOME FUN

When guys approach you, have fun with it. You don't have to marry him. You don't have to date him. You don't even have to be his friend or continue the conversation after the first thirty seconds if you don't want to, but whatever you do, don't be intentionally boring or uninteresting. Is being boring and uninteresting fun for you? Is it fun for your friends? While most of the guys that approach you can likely be eliminated almost immediately, it doesn't mean you can't have fun with their approaches. Interact with them, smile, tease and be challenging in a fun way. Get out of your head and be conscious of what is going on around you. Don't attach too much meaning to any one guy who approaches. You never know when Mr. Right will approach. For all you know, he could be the next guy you speak to, so make sure you make the most of each interaction. You'll be happier and will have more fun as a result!

Here is an example of a typical boring conversation that may take place:

Dylin: Hi, I'm Dylin

Maria: ummm…hi

Dylin: Are you from around here?

Maria: Yes

Dylin: What do you do for fun?

Maria: Nothing really

Dylin: What do you do for work?

Maria: I work at the hospital

Dylin: What are you doing today?

Maria: I have to go

While Dylin's attempts to initiate conversation are painfully boring, this is a common way for people to start conversations. It seems logical for the guy, and he won't be having any more fun than you are in this case. Probably less, as he's nervous. He very well may be this boring, but then again, he may not be. When someone talking to you is boring, it may be your natural reaction to be boring back. You can find out if the guy is a dud very quickly by having a little more fun with the interaction. It is not your obligation or responsibility to make 'him' more fun or interesting, but it is your responsibility to have more fun yourself.

Let's look at the conversation again when the woman tries to have more fun with it:

Dylin: Hi, I'm Dylin

Maria: What up Dylin? I'm Maria (shaking his hand with some cheesy, lame-ass, but oh so funny handshake)

Dylin: What was that? (smiling)

Maria: Oh, nothing. I'm a bit of a nut (big smile)

Dylin: Are you from around here?

Maria: Right here? No, I am just vacationing in this particular spot. I make my primary residence closer to the bar.

> Dylin: Oh yes, this is more like the suburbs where the bar is more like downtown. It's where the fun is, but nice to get out of town once and a while as well. Do you work around here as well? Closer to the rest rooms perhaps?
>
> Maria: hahaha… I actually get out of town to work! I am a registered nurse over at the hospital. I take sick people and I un-sick them! Bwaaa-haa ha ha (laughing at her own cheesy joke).

Do you see how the same boring conversation can be turned around so both have more fun with it? It makes the whole situation a little more light hearted while taking the pressure off. The interaction now becomes two people having fun. In this case, Dylin turned out to be pretty cool and was able to convey his personality as well. He could have just as easily continued to be King Super Bore (Let's call it KSB for short), in which case Maria could just say, "well, it was nice meeting you Dylin, I'm going to talk to my friends now." She turns her back to him and returns to her friends. No need for rudeness. No need for more of an explanation. She allowed herself to have more fun in that situation, which sets the frame for her to have more fun for the rest of the evening. She just increased her chances of finding Mr. Right by 1000% (of course, that 1000% is clinically proven and scientifically tested to be 100% accurate).

Here is another example of a common scenario where the guy is interesting but the woman is intentionally boring:

> Brandon is an attractive guy who walks over: OMG, the funniest thing just happened to me. I was outside and this woman asked me if I was Pee Wee Herman! I think she was serious! Do I really look like Pee Wee?
>
> Sarah: No
>
> Brandon: Oh, thank you so much for the reassurance! I was starting to wrongfully question my divinely handsome good looks. Now I can sleep tonight with confidence.
>
> Sarah: Good for you.
>
> Brandon: Come on, smile! It goes like this: (gives a big cheesy smile while pointing to it with both hands as a demonstration).
>
> Sarah: (gives a half assed attempt coming off as a 'F You' smirk. Sarah then turns back to talk to her friends).

Good for you Sarah. You just told Mr. Right to get lost, and you are in less of a good mood now as a result (and probably weren't in the best of moods before either). Brandon was a fun guy and could have been everything she was looking for. Now she'll never know.

You are not going to be interested in every guy that approaches and you will no doubt encounter a lot of losers. Just have more fun with each one and look for the ways to see the humor in each and every guy that approaches you. When you are having more fun, just watch how many more great men you will meet.

WHAT'S STOPPING YOU FROM APPROACHING HIM?

While there is an old fashioned rule out there that says men need to do all the approaching, does that mean you have to adhere to such an archaic belief?

Who says you can't go up and start a conversation with him? It happens all the time. It doesn't have to be aggressive, asking him out or even asking for his phone number. That part, you can let him handle. But you can certainly get his attention and there is nothing wrong with that! What stops you from walking over to him in the grocery store and telling him that you like his smile? Or his jacket? Or commenting on the fact that he has Nestlé Quik chocolate syrup in his cart? (mmmmmm Nestlé Quik). You can tell him that you love Quik and ask him if it is for his kids or for the kid inside of him? All you have to do here is initiate the conversation. It also wouldn't hurt to give some sort of indication that you are actually interested in him and not just his Quik.

Another great way would be for you to ask for his opinion about something. Men love being asked our opinion by women, (we often love to give it regardless). It is a great way to approach that is both easy and non-threatening. If you don't like the way he answered or the way he looks once you see him up close, it is very easy to bail after he gives you his opinion. Just say thanks and walk away. If you do like him, make sure you give a strong signal so he knows you are not just interested in whether you should buy the Civic or the Mustang (personally, I'd take the Mustang).

Women will typically get approached much more than men do. After all, it is society's perception that men are the ones who do the approaching. As a result, women become more adept in situations where they are getting approached, as they have been through it many more times than the man has. This can give you the upper hand in these situations as the onus is on him to continue the conversation and follow through with some sort of close. Whether it be asking you for your number or meeting up somewhere afterwards.

ATTRACT, DON'T CHASE

To paraphrase the movie The Matrix, you will open the door for him, but he has to walk through it. Once you have approached and given him some kind of noticeable hint that you are interested, it is up to him to take it from there. Don't make it too easy for him. Once you have approached him you can then back away and let him pursue. Men like to be the pursuers, so don't deprive him of that. You have to attract, not chase. You have done your part. Keep it fun as I mentioned earlier and don't be afraid to tease him a little. What kind of an adult drinks Nestlé Quik anyway? If a woman were to playfully make fun of me for having it in my shopping cart, I would certainly love it.

Never be afraid to initiate conversation. Men are very easy to talk to and we are almost always open to meeting you. We LOVE when we don't have to do the initial approach! It might seem a little terrifying at first, but there are some very easy tools that I will provide for you that will virtually eliminate your fear to allow you to approach him with ease. Are you ready for them?

"You can't be that kid at the top of the waterslide overthinking it. You have to go down the chute."
~Tina Fey

TACKLING YOUR FEAR

First of all, you need to understand that men are generally very easy to talk to. We don't get women approaching us very often, so it is a nice surprise and quite flattering when they do, even if they are not our type. You will be super surprised at just how friendly we can be! The most important thing to realize in eliminating any fear is to approach without any expectations. You aren't 'hitting on him' so to speak, you are just being fun and asking him why the hell he has Quik in his shopping cart. It could also be to tell him that you simply like his shirt, or whatever it may be. As a follow up question you can ask him if he is from the area. Don't worry about being boring with your follow up questions. Just get him started in conversation and let him work it from there. You will be able to get an idea of his personality in less than a minute or two. Let him carry the conversation, as he should be able to do. It is part of him pursuing you. If he just stares back at you in silence with a stupid, dimwitted look on his face, then just tell him it was nice meeting him and walk away.

You will be proud of yourself for doing this. If you are fearful, then doing this exercise will build a tremendous amount of self-confidence pretty much instantly. The more fearful you were at the beginning, the more proud of yourself you will be and the more self-confidence you will build.

When you go out of your comfort zone, growth takes place and confidence is built. Whatever happens, just don't attach too much meaning to it. Have fun with it, and don't forget to smile. I'll be talking more about fear in Chapter Eleven.

THE SOUL MATE YOU NEVER MEET

".....I decided to marry her. Courtship would be a mere formality. But what to say to begin the courtship? 'Would you like some gum?' seemed too low-class. "Hello," was too trite a greeting for my future bride. "I love you! I am hot with passion!" seemed too forward. "I want to make you the mother of my children," seemed a bit premature.

Nothing. That's right, I said nothing, And after awhile, the bus reached her stop, she got off, and I never saw her again. End of story"

~Allan Garner,
quoted from his book
'Conversationally Speaking'.

I am confident that situations like this happen thousands or tens of thousands times per day in this world. You see someone who you think looks perfect for you, and nothing ever happens. How do you know that person isn't your future husband? I can't tell you how many times I have been out over the years and I have seen women that I would have loved to talk to, but it never happened. I made some sort of excuse for not approaching her. "She looks in a rush, she doesn't look friendly, she is too tall, too short, she probably has a boyfriend, I have no idea what to say, what if I am boring, what if she rejects me, what if she doesn't like me?

What if she has a boyfriend that is standing ten feet away?" These are all the things that used to go through my head. Were they justified? Of the hundreds (or even thousands) that I didn't end up approaching over twenty plus years, I'll never ever know. The ones I did approach? Sometimes they *were* justified. Sometimes I was boring, sometimes she didn't like me, and sometimes she had a boyfriend who WAS standing only ten feet away! Were the situations sometimes uncomfortable? Definitely they were, but I survived to fight another day. There were also many times when they weren't justified at all, and the interaction went well. The negative thoughts going through my mind were nothing but thoughts. How many great women did I miss out on meeting by listening to figments of my imagination?

What every single interaction had in common was that I was always proud of myself for making the effort, regardless of the outcome. The first time I started walking up to women in the daytime, I was scared out of my wits, but I ended up building large amounts of self-confidence fast by acting in spite of this fear.

I'm of course very thankful for my experience now and thankful for all the missed approaches. They brought me to Kelly, and I can't imagine anyone else being more perfect for me.

If you see a guy you like, you owe it to yourself, and to him, to give him some kind of approach signal. I remember a time WAY back when I was in college, a girl in my class who I used to talk to frequently was always fun and friendly. Then one day, all of a sudden, she was aloof and a little snippy towards me whenever I would say anything. It was a phase that lasted for only a couple of weeks. A few months later, we ended up dating and I asked her what that was all about. She said she was mad because I hadn't made a move. If you like someone that you interact with regularly, it's time to make sure he knows you are interested in him as more than just a friend or he might not see it.

There was another time I was working at a four-day trade show in Las Vegas when I met a girl named Teri. We said a few words to each other over the next few days and joked around with her, as I did with the other exhibitors like I always do. She never really said much to me, or gave me any sort of indication that she was even slightly interested. If anything, I found her a little aloof. After the show was over, I found out that she was totally into me and was waiting for me to make a move. Hello? How the hell would I know that? She wasn't really my type, but if I had known that, I may have asked her out for a drink afterwards and see what happened from there.

Another time back in college, there was a girl named Stella that sat across from me in one of my classes for an entire semester. She was quite quiet and never really said much. I later found out that she would journal about me regularly and wished I would talk to her. If I had known this, there is no telling what would have happened. Maybe it would have turned into something, maybe it wouldn't have, but now we will never know.

As I specified earlier, make it easier for him to approach you by giving a noticeable signal or do the approach yourself.

SEARCHING FOR COMMONALITIES

When men initiate conversation, the first thing they will typically do is try to search for commonalities to use as fuel for the conversation. To men, this is the logical way to start a conversation and this is the way men communicate with each other. They don't realize that women typically won't want to build comfort with some stranger they just met. Searching for commonalities usually takes the form of 'How are you? What do you do? What's your name? Where are you from?' There is another word that can be used for this type of approach and that word is BORRRING! After all, don't you want Mr. Right to just come in and sweep you off your feet? Mr. Right is FAR from boring! In a setting like a bar or nightclub, it can be down right annoying to women.

Several years ago when I was out a bar with a friend in Kansas City, I naturally started chatting with a couple of girls. After about five minutes of my razzling and dazzling, she stopped me mid-sentence and said "You're asking very eclectic questions. I mean, this isn't your typical 'bar' conversation." While I have no recollection of what I was actually saying to her, I do remember what followed:

> "What would you rather I start with? Hi, how are you, what do you do, where are you from?"
>
> "Oh my god, I HAAATE that!"
>
> "Exactly."

Guys are really quite clueless and fail to realize just how boring this is to most women. As most attractive women will get hit on often when they are out in public (especially if they are out at a bar or club), they talk to a lot of men. Most of these men end up having the same conversations over and over, to the point where both parties start to get frustrated. To most men, they don't get approached too frequently, if at all, so they really don't understand just how boring they are coming across. They want to meet you. This doesn't mean they are 'interested' in you. After all, you really haven't given them any reason to be at this point. While a lot of these guys may seem a little on the dull side at first (and some of them are), this doesn't necessarily mean that they are not the guy that you are looking for.

In an ideal world, Mr. Right would have the perfect thing to say. It is not every day that a three legged dog walks by or you see woman throwing a fit at Whole Foods that would give him something situational to base the conversation on. He needs to create something, so he turns to what is logical.

What's ironic is that even though this type of conversation building can be a turn off in a lot of cases (okay, in most cases), this is exactly what women will tend to do when they try to start a conversation with a guy that they like.

TEASING WITH COMMONALITIES

It is a little different on your end, as searching for commonalities with men is acceptable. Ask questions about things he might be interested in, as this will give you an opportunity to find out what he is like and takes some of the pressure off him. Don't be afraid to playfully tease him about his answers. This is how you can make the otherwise boring search for commonalities fun and interesting. Teasing is fun, playful, and shows personality. Just be careful that you aren't being mean, as it's a fine line. Can this backfire? Anything can happen, after all, different people have different personalities and some may be a little more sensitive than others. If he doesn't like it then he is probably not for you anyway. Playfully teasing is the foundation of flirting, not to mention, loads of fun!

Here are some examples:

- You ask what he does and he says he is in the pharmaceutical industry. Your response, "Oh, so you are a drug dealer?"
- He is an accountant – "Wow, you must be a blast at parties!"
- You ask him where he is from and he says Nebraska. Your response, "That's awesome! Did you have to milk cows and churn butter before school?"
- You ask what he likes to do for fun and he says he loves to play golf. You can say, "Me too, but it's so frustrating as the last time I played, I couldn't get the ball past the big windmill!"

In the last example he started talking about golf and you purposely misinterpreted it to mean mini-golf. It's a cute and fun response that will probably make him laugh. The idea here is to be playful and funny at the same time.

MISINTERPRETING INTENTIONS

Mike was out with some friends one evening when he met a stunning German exchange student named Tanja. They spoke for hours and had a great connection. She was hanging on every word he said and vice versa. It was the middle of summer and Mike and some of his friends were going to the beach the next day. Since they were getting along so well, he thought why not invite her along? Since she had arrived only a few days before, Mike asked her if she had a bikini to wear at the beach. Their interaction went downhill from there. In her eyes, that was a very rude question to ask. He tried to explain himself by saying that he wasn't sure if she would have packed any swimwear as Canada is known for ice and snow, not so much beaches, sun tanning and swimming. She didn't care what he had to say at that point. It was rude question and that was that. They never saw each other again.

Mike was just asking a question, which seemed quite logical. Tanja however attached her own meaning to his comments and then accepted it as fact. No explanations accepted. She didn't want to hear it. The more Mike tried to explain himself, the lower his value became. There isn't much Mike could have done as it was his logic vs. her emotions, and a woman's emotions will win every time. What many men simply do not understand is that they need to try to change a woman's mood, not try to change her mind. Trying to change a woman's mind can be like trying to fix your bruised thumb by continually hitting it with a hammer. By trying to change her mind, all Mike was doing was making her angry and further digging his own grave.

COMPLIMENTS...GOOD OR BAD?

While women make many of their choices based on emotion, men make their choices based on logic. This is something that very few men have figured out and will try to engage and captivate women by doing what makes sense to them. This leads to a lot of frustration for many men because women's brains are wired so differently from ours. For example, guys might start off by giving compliments, as this seems logical to them. After all, they would love for a woman to walk up to them and start flattering them. While everyone enjoys receiving sincere compliments, they have their time and their place. The more attractive a particular woman is, the more compliments she will naturally receive. This can start to get downright annoying for women in settings like bars or nightclubs where approaching is socially acceptable and typical.

For example, let's say you are out at a bar with a group of your girlfriends. You just want to have a good time with your friends but you keep getting interrupted:

Random guy 1: Wow, you are gorgeous
Girl: Oh, thank you!

Random guy 2: You are the most beautiful girl in here
Girl: Great, thanks!

Random guy 3: OMG, you are hot!
Girl: Thanks

Random guy 4: Damn, you are gorgeous! I'm Steve
Girl: Ummm… thank you

Random guy 5: Wow, you are beautiful!
Girl: (Silently nods and turns back to her friends)

Random guy 6: Yo yo yo girl, you is fine!
Girl: Whatever

This barrage of compliments will get so boring and stale, that you can't help but turn away all these men. Some of these guys may be great, but because they have no 'game' you have no 'interest.'

This type of approaching doesn't create any emotion with women. It is also pretty transparent. However, this doesn't mean the guy approaching is a 'bad guy', or not right for her, yet his value does drop in her mind regardless of how great he may be.

If you like a guy, definitely give him compliments! Remember, regardless of how good looking the guy may be, he doesn't get anywhere near as many compliments as an equally attractive woman would receive (not even close!). It isn't that hard to impress him this way, but this too is a fine line. Just tread lightly and don't come on too strongly. If you aren't getting compliments back, then refrain from giving them. Quid pro quo. Don't give him any more than what he is giving you. This doesn't just apply when you first meet someone. It applies right through the entire relationship.

WHY MEN TALK ABOUT THEMSELVES

As men typically do most of the approaching, we also have to carry the bulk of the conversation in the early stages. For men, this presents a challenge. Not only do we have to work up the courage to approach, we also have to carry on a witty, (sometimes one-sided) conversation as well. When a random guy approaches, you may be thinking, "who is this guy and why should I make an effort?" The guy knows it may take a bit of work to get you interested in him, so he will need to subtly, 'sell' himself to you. He feels he has to win you over, but he also has to be careful he doesn't come across as bragging. It is a bit of a catch twenty-two.

This is why men talk about themselves. We know we have to get you interested in us if we are to have a shot. Most men however don't realize that talking too much about themselves can be a turn off to many women. They want to show that they are good enough to be a potential mate. In many cases, they are also just trying to keep the conversation going.

While you may think he is a little self-centered, he is simply doing this because he is interested in you, which is why he is making an effort. Men don't understand that this is generally not what women want, but women should try to recognize this as flattery and not as a large negative strike against the guy. Many men don't realize that after attempting to demonstrate his value, they need to start asking the woman open-ended questions to get her to talk. This will give him a better chance of impressing the woman and shows that he actually is interested in her and not just in himself.

If it seems like a guy is talking a lot about himself, try jumping into the conversation and recite a quick story that relates to what he is saying. Conversation isn't just about asking questions. When a woman is silent, a guy will assume that she doesn't have anything to say and may keep talking. While you might feel it is rude to interrupt by jumping in with a point or a story of your own, this is completely acceptable in conversation and helps with chemistry. If a guy is talking to you, he is interested. He is talking because he is trying to win you over. The more active of a role you play in the conversation, the better the interaction will go and the more he will like you.

JUDGING

Many women I know and have dated in the past seem to have adopted the term 'judging.' This is really not something that most men use too often but women seem to think people are judging them all the time.

'Are you judging me?'

Whenever this goes through your mind when first meeting someone, the answer is often yes. You are being judged. But don't look at this as a bad thing. The guy doesn't know who you are, so naturally he is going to form some conclusions about you, just as you will with him. Everything you do is going to leave an impression on him, good or bad. Whether you realize it or not, you too are judging people all the time. Everytime a guy approaches you, you are immediately going to judge him on his looks, his body language, his mannerisms, and on everything he says. People judge each other, and they always will whether you like it or not. It is human nature.

Most commonly, people judge based on appearances. If you are walking down a quiet street and you see a guy wearing torn jeans with the crotch around his knees, tattoos down each arm, a shaved head and piercings in his lip, nose, eyebrow, etc. On the other side of the street you see a guy wearing an Armani suit with a fresh haircut and a Prada attaché case. Are you going to have different thoughts about each one? What if you were looking at buying a home and you were interviewing real estate agents and your only two options were as described above, but you knew the first one was more qualified. Would you still select him? Unlikely! You are judging. While this is an extreme example, it rings true in other areas as well.

Still don't like the term 'judging?' Try rereading the above paragraph but this time replace the word 'judge' with 'evaluate' and see if you feel differently.

SILENCE YOUR AUTO RESPONSE

Whenever I get a telemarketing call, I have a response that automatically comes out as if it was preprogrammed into my brain. "Not interested thanks," followed by loud bang as I slam the phone down abruptly (hard to create this same effect with a smart phone!) Women who get approached by men regularly also tend to have auto responses. For example, a guy may approach and you spurt out, "I have a boyfriend" when you don't. Subconsciously you may want to talk to the person, but your internal auto responder prevents you from doing so. You may come across as cold, aloof or just flat out not interested. Be conscious of your auto responses as they may be limiting your success by cutting guys short a little too quickly. If you like the way a guy looks, and his body language is congruent with his speech, then give him a moment before spouting out the auto response. Since the auto response is in fact 'auto', you may blurt it out without even thinking. So take a moment to continue the conversation with him before being so quick with the dreaded auto response, if you choose to do so.

COMFORT BUILDING

Once mutual attraction has been established, you move into comfort building. At this stage, you are further building your rapport and are starting to establish a connection with each other through casual conversation. There is no pressure for sex or anything else during this phase. You are merely learning about each others likes, your dislikes, hobbies, interests, values, past experiences, and are establishing commonalities. The least amount of pressure is felt at this stage as all you are doing is having a conversation. The primary objective of comfort building is to learn about each other and determine if there is more substance in your connection beyond the original attraction. You are basically getting to know one another better.

Comfort building can take longer than all the other phases as there is much more involved. This phase will continue all the way through until you are in a committed relationship. However, without solid comfort building, it is unlikely you will want to see him again.

Comfort is also about building trust. You aren't going to give your number to someone who you don't trust, so you are naturally going to want to feel a certain comfort level before you do so. As you start to feel somewhat comfortable with each other, you may come to the conclusion that you want to explore the opportunity further. It is at this time when you exchange numbers.

EXCHANGING NUMBERS

You get to the point in the interaction where you like him, but he hasn't asked for your number yet. A guy should really have the balls to go for the close, whether it is asking for a number or for an email. If he doesn't, it doesn't necessarily mean he doesn't like you. He could have been looking for that perfect time to ask, which may never come. Perhaps you were interrupted by a friend or phone call. If he felt the slightest bit rushed then he may not have felt comfortable asking. There are a lot of quality men out there that are not very good at this stuff who may let the interaction pass without getting your number. He may be kicking himself for it afterwards, and probably is if he thought it went well. You can ask for his number if you want, but just make sure you back away after you get things started. You will need to let him chase. Don't get into a situation where you are chasing him! If you feel he had plenty of opportunity to ask for your number, but failed to do so, then I would let it go.

Chapter Seven Highlights

- ✓ If a guy is smooth, he most likely has lots of experience with women and has done this many times before. He may be a player, but always take the time to find out for sure before labeling and rejecting him. He may be going through all those women just to find you.
- ✓ It is not easy for a man to approach women, and if he doesn't do it regularly, then it is only natural for him to feel anxiety and may not be his true self

- ✓ Don't give subtle hints that you like a guy. It doesn't work as men won't pick up on it. Give large, obvious hints.
- ✓ It can be difficult for anyone, men or women, to come up with the perfect thing to say right off the bat. If he seems a little boring at first, just have fun with it. Tease him a little and be playful. You are having fun for YOU, not for HIM. This makes for a more light-hearted situation and allows him to open up and show you who he really is.
- ✓ You never know when the next guy to approach you might be Mr. Right.
- ✓ It's okay for you to approach men.
- ✓ Attract men, but never chase them.
- ✓ Men will try to find commonalities before building attraction, which can be boring. You can have fun with it and turn the conversation from boring to fun, even if it is just for your own benefit.
- ✓ Don't give more compliments then you receive. Quid pro quo.
- ✓ Men need to 'sell' themselves to you as they need to build value for themselves. This is how they get you to like them.
- ✓ People will naturally judge you and judge each other. Get over it.
- ✓ Silence your auto responses
- ✓ If he doesn't ask for your number, you can ask him. Just don't chase once the contact has been made.
- ✓ Comfort building is where you learn more about each

other and determine if there may be something of substance to base an actual relationship on.

Now that you have each others contact info, the waiting game begins!

CHAPTER EIGHT

WAITING

BETWEEN MEETING AND THE FIRST DATE

"Learn to relax. Your body is precious, as it houses your mind and spirit. Inner peace begins with a relaxed body."
~Norman Vincent Peale

So now you have met him, established a mutual attraction for one another and decided you are going to meet up for a date. Personally, I like to get a date set up right after the initial meeting and then exchange info to finalize the details. However, most guys are not going to do this, as they just go for the number at first. Once you have exchanged numbers, someone has to take action.

TEXTING

These days, texting has become the preferred method of communication after meeting someone. It is non-threatening and less time consuming than a call. With a phone call, you have to drop everything you are doing so you can focus on the conversation. With texting, you can continue doing whatever you were doing and can still maintain a conversation. Boy, was I wrong when I said this texting thing would never catch on! This doesn't mean that you should never talk to him on the phone though. He really should pick it up at some point and call you so he can hear your voice, but don't get upset if he doesn't. If he doesn't call, it doesn't mean he doesn't care, isn't interested, or thinks any less of you.

When he texts you, you can text him back right away if you like, but don't seem too eager. For example, if you met a guy you like at a grocery store, you could always initiate a text saying something like, "it was nice meeting you this afternoon next to the bananas." (Providing of course that you did in fact meet him next to the bananas!) I still remember when I met Catalina at Walmart, (yes, I would pick up there too) it just happened to be in the pharmacy section and right in front of the condoms. This made for some fun and attraction building humor by text. "It was nice meeting you in front of the condoms. Hope you found what you were looking for." The fun and witty banter that followed and gave us an inside joke that I always referred back to throughout our relationship.

Timing of texts

When I was dating Rhonda, sometimes I would take two or

three hours to respond to her. It wasn't that I didn't like her or wanted to play games. Sometimes I just needed some space and other times I was legitimately busy. As soon as I would respond, she would text me back IMMEDIATELY. Every time. Not only did this become annoying, it made her seem super needy and was quite a turn off. I actually remember rolling my eyes every time this happened. Remember, men like to do a bit of chasing. With her always texting me back immediately, I never had the chance. She was always the first one to text. Always. While this is flattering for a bit, it is not a way to hook a guy. It has the opposite effect. The fact that I never had to do any chasing with Rhonda ended up killing my attraction for her, which is too bad, because I really did like her otherwise.

As a general rule of thumb, if you text a guy and he doesn't respond for ten minutes, then take at least the same amount of time to respond. If he takes an hour, then take an hour. Match his response time. The point is not to play games, it is to avoid coming across as too eager. After all, you have a life and are not always free to text him back immediately. If he is busy doing other things and can't text you back right away, then you should be busy doing other things as well.

MISUNDERSTANDINGS

A few years ago I was out at a bar in New York City with my good friend Pete when he met a girl named Holly. They really hit it off and had a lot of fun that night. He was definitely interested in seeing her again. They exchanged many playful texts and it was clear there was a lot of chemistry. Pete is a doctor and that was something Holly found attractive about him. However, it didn't take too long before she started to question whether he really was a doctor or not, so she decided to test him. She texted, "If you are really a doctor, then what is the largest muscle in the human body?" Pete is a pretty playful guy and is always looking for ways to have fun and turn something into a joke. His response was the "cremaster muscle." This is of course far from the right answer. It is something that most people wouldn't know about unless they had a strong knowledge of the human anatomy. Someone like say….. a doctor. Anyone who is familiar with this muscle would know that it isn't even close to being in the running for the largest muscle! It's primary function is what makes it a funny answer. (It's a small muscle in men that flexes their scrotum.) Her response was, "Never text me again."

Pete was trying to be funny and also gave an answer that only a doctor could possibly know. It appeared as though she viewed it as if he didn't know the answer and was therefore lying about being a doctor. Would they have ended up together? We'll never know because Holly misunderstood Pete's sense of humor and what he was trying to get across. If she had played along a little, things may have been different. One thing I can say for sure is that Holly missed the opportunity to date a great guy who she had established a connection with.

The moral of the story is that if a guy texts you something that makes you mad or pushes the wrong button, take a moment to figure out if you are interpreting the text correctly. Look at the text and come up with a few different options for what he could have possibly meant. Text him back again to find out. This has to be done carefully as you don't want to scare him away if you did in fact take it wrong. Holly could have responded with something as simple as "I really don't think that is the biggest muscle in the human body," to which Pete would have then clarified his response. It can be as simple as that. Don't let a potential Mr. Right slip through your fingers just because you misinterpreted one of his texts.

WHAT ABOUT CALLING?

There are some really strange beliefs out there about women calling men. Generally, the woman shouldn't be the one to call. Why? If you want to call him then call him. As long as you let him do most of the chasing and don't seem too eager, there is nothing wrong with you calling him. Natalie called me and I ended up entering a three year relationship with her. Don't call him too frequently though. I had a girl call me twenty-seven times in one day once. This goes without saying, but that is beyond an example of too frequently!

Mike was out one Saturday night when he met Melissa. The two talked for about thirty minutes when they decided to exchange numbers. Melissa had the bartender get her a pen so she could write his number down (this was before everyone had a cell phone). Mike called her on Monday, but he unfortunately got her voicemail so he left a message. Two days went by yet Mike didn't get a return call. He tried again on Wednesday night and got her voicemail once again. Just as before, Mike left a message for her and once again, no return call. That was it for Mike. He wasn't going to try again. The next night he came home and happened to see her number on his call display, so he thought he would try her a third time. This time she picked up. On their date, Melissa revealed that she had told her father about Mike and that she really liked him. Her father encouraged her to call him back, although she was too chicken to leave a voicemail when she did. She wasn't going to call him back because she was too shy and if it wasn't for her father's advice and a little luck, they never would have got together.

If you like him, make sure you call him back as most guys won't try more than once. If you happen to miss his call, it is perfectly okay to call him back right away. As guys, it is not uncommon for women to give us their numbers just to get rid of us. Or they may have every intention of talking to us further at the time they give us their number, but then they run cold. As men, we are used to women giving us their number and then never returning our calls or texts (of course that has never happened to me, 'smile'). If you are interested, let him know by at least texting him back as it is important that he knows you are at least somewhat interested.

Don't worry if he doesn't ask you out on the first call. He may do this during a follow up call or by text. Guys who have options with women may not ask you out during the initial call, so don't put too much emphasis on it. Just as he doesn't ask you out during the initial call, you don't have to necessarily jump at meeting up with him after the first call either. You are busy with a life of your own and it can be beneficial to show him that. Never be too available. Again, show him you have a life of your own and he will respect you all that much more for it.

This also means you should never be sitting by the phone waiting for him to call. Doing this is just setting you up for failure as it will drive you crazy and make it all that much harder to be yourself. Go out there and do what you would normally be doing. Have fun and enjoy life. There will be plenty of time for you to talk to this person. As hard as it may be when you like someone, it is very important to keep yourself busy. Keeping yourself busy is much better than just sitting by the phone like a dillweed making yourself a nervous wreck… which is not going to accomplish anything positive.

GAIN SOME POWER

Want to gain a bit of power and have a bit of an upper hand? Be the first to end the call, especially if it is going well. This will drive him nuts thinking about you! I'm not talking about after hours of conversation. I'm talking about after five or ten minutes of good conversation. Leave him wanting more and he will start to give chase. Men secretly love this, though most won't admit it. If they like you even a little bit, they will like you a lot more if they have to put a bit of effort into getting you.

WHY GUYS DON'T CALL

Women may find themselves in a situation where the guy just doesn't seem to be that interested, yet they try all that much harder to get him, then wonder why he doesn't call. Never make a big deal over a guy not calling. It is going to happen from time to time. Sometimes we just need some time and space to let our intuition guide us and we may end up deciding not to call at all. I have been guilty of asking a girl for her number and then never calling. So why did I do this? Sometimes I may have been borderline as to whether I wanted to see her again, other times it may have been alcohol induced. I can remember one specific time where I really wanted to call but didn't end up calling. Why? Because it was the new era of smart phones and I had just got my new BlackBerry and apparently didn't know how to save numbers! DOH! Whatever the reason, don't attach too much meaning to a guy who you barely know not calling. It sucks sometimes. As guys, we go through it regularly!

If a guy takes his time in calling you or calling you back, creating confrontation when he does call is going to result in the opposite of what you want. If a guy doesn't call you for an extended period (such as a month), then he is not interested. Sure, it is possible that he lost his address book, his dog was sick, or he was abducted by aliens, but most likely, its that he is just not into you. Confronting for not calling will never result in anything good and will just put up barriers. So don't do it. Sometimes he may come to his senses after a week or two… or longer, and will then want to call. If there has been a lot of time in between and you want to call him, there is nothing wrong with doing this. You never know what might happen. That being said, I have to admonish you once again. Don't chase! I'm talking about a single call, not multiple calls. Once you get his attention, you then need to pull back and let him chase you. I know I am being repetitive, but I really can't stress this enough.

UNCERTAINTY

Sometimes you meet men that you aren't quite sure about. You don't know him that well, and the initial interest you had in him may have waned a little by now. Do you go out with him? Do you not go out with him? Do you return his texts or just ignore him all together? The key thing here is how you felt about him when you first met him. You did in fact give him your number so you were considering a possibility of meeting up with him when you met.

No one says you have to go out with him right away (or even at all). Let him chase a bit. Is he able to make you laugh or smile with his texts? Is he at least somewhat interesting? If the answer to that is no, then it is unlikely he will be fun on a date. If you are unsure, this is a perfect example of a time when you may just want to leave it as it is and let it fade out. If his texts are fun, interesting and entertaining and you are still a little unsure then you have to ask yourself why. Maybe it would still be worth meeting up with him to see how you feel when you see him again. It doesn't have to occupy a whole evening or be anything too extensive. Even coffee or a quick drink is fine. You just want to see if you feel any sort of chemistry when you meet up again. If thirty minutes goes by and still nothing, then go ahead and bail. This is the magic of the coffee date. Let him know it is going to be something quick as you have a lot of things to do. It gives you a quick in and out. If you both want to prolong the date, then that option exists as well. If you are borderline as to whether you would like to see him again, then the coffee date is kind of a happy medium. Don't look at it as a 'date', just look at it as a meet up. Still not sure? Talk to him on the phone. Being interesting by text is one thing, but being interesting on the phone is another. See how you feel after a real conversation without either of you hiding behind your device.

ASKING HIM OUT

The old fashioned way of thinking is that the man should always be the one to ask the woman out. While I do believe the guy should be the one doing the vast majority of the chasing, there are times when the woman can go ahead and ask the guy out as well. I'm not talking about the traditional, "Hey, what are you doing Friday night? Would you like to get together?" There is a much better way of asking someone out that is more 'off the radar' and doesn't quite seem so obvious.

The best way to ask someone out is to see if they are available to accompany at something that you would be doing anyway. "I am going to this 'ugly painting' exhibit at the art gallery this weekend, you should come along." Or, "I am going to see this great band on Friday night, you should come!" By asking someone out this way and by limiting it to more non-conventional dates, you can remove a lot of the typical dating pressure that comes with asking someone out. It also can alleviate the fear of rejection, as the context is that you are going to be doing this thing anyway, with or without him. If he says no, then oh well, you are going anyway and are going to have a good time with or without him. These types of dates are great ways to build comfort as well! By being more relaxed, both of you will find it much easier than being on an 'interview' type date, and I guarantee you'll have more fun!

Chapter Eight Highlights

- ✓ If you text a guy and he takes awhile to return your text, take at least the same amount of time to text him back.
- ✓ If a guy calls you, make sure you call him back if you like him. There are many quality guys that won't try calling more than once and will just assume you aren't interested.
- ✓ Don't jump to conclusions over a single text. Always take it at least a few texts further to ensure you understood him correctly.
- ✓ If you are uncertain about seeing him again and are sitting on the fence, opt for a simple and more informal date such as meeting for coffee. If you decide you don't want to continue, you can escape quickly.
- ✓ You can ask a guy out and assuage the fear of rejection by inviting him along on something you are going to be doing anyway.
- ✓ If you are going to ask him out or give suggestions, try for something more non-traditional

You now have your first date set up and it is time to start getting ready for it. Let's make sure you put your best foot forward to give it the highest possibility of success.

CHAPTER NINE

THE FIRST DATE

"Be who you are and say what you feel,
because those who mind don't matter
and those who matter don't mind."
~Dr. Seuss

On your first date your number one goal should be to determine if the two of you have chemistry. In fact, the best first date will end with the two of you knowing nothing about each other. The chemistry you had was so strong that you never even really got around to asking each other any questions. Your first date doesn't have to be like this for things to work out great, but it sure is a good start if it does. While these dates are fun and good at establishing that the two of you have great chemistry, you also need to start looking for ways to begin communicating.

If you are fortunate, you will have a situation as described above, but you certainly don't need to go through the whole date discussing nothing but jibber jabber for you to realize there is chemistry. You can ask questions and ask questions you should! Just make sure you keep it fun and keep the serious questions to a minimum. Guys know that most women out there are looking for commitment. They may hint that they are looking for commitment as well, but say they want to take it slow at the beginning. Or they may say they want commitment, but their actions become more evasive as you continue to date them. A guy hinting that he is looking for a relationship can also be a trick to get what he wants from you, so be careful.

This is why the first date is a great time to start communicating *a little*, as long as you keep it light. You don't want to start dumping on your exes or telling him about your problems. NOT a good idea! Be fun, remember? He isn't your therapist. This would be another sure-fire way to catch the last train to Singleville.

You don't want to come across as you interrogating him, and you also want to try to avoid making it seem like an interview. Just as in a job interview where the interviewer wants to find out if you would be a fit for the position you are applying for, you want to find out if your date is going to be a fit for your life.

This is why it is important that you dig deep in the exercises found throughout this book. The better you understand your own thoughts, the better chance you have of finding the perfect guy.

DON'T TAKE IT SO SERIOUSLY!

When it comes to dating, you really can't take any one date too seriously. If it goes well, then by all means give it some extra attention, but you don't want to start looking at it as something that it is not. Don't have yourself married to him in your mind. Don't start thinking of a future with him in any way at this point. It's just a date! Instead of looking at all your dates so seriously, try taking more of an unserious, nonchalant kind of approach. This will take off a tremendous amount of pressure and will make it easier for you to just loosen up, go with the flow, and enjoy yourself.

GAINING APPROVAL

On the first date, it is only natural to want to make a good impression, which is fine, but you have to ensure you remain true to who you are. This means being 100% honest with not only him, but also with yourself. Honesty is one of the key components to success in any relationship, so you want to start forming this habit right from the beginning. Don't do or say anything that contradicts who you are or what you believe in, just to get him to like you. Another way of saying this is DON'T LIE! For example, if he says he loves football, don't tell him you love it too if you really can't stand it. Be honest. If it doesn't work out, then it doesn't work out. The first date shouldn't be about how you can make it work with this one particular guy, it should be about determining your compatibility with one another. If you're not compatible then wouldn't you rather find out now? This is what first dates are for! Leverage them to your advantage to get your relationship off to a good start by forming solid roots. Don't start forming habits of lying or they will become harder to break as the relationship progresses. Do you want to get yourself into a relationship with someone who is just 'okay' for you, while at the same time he thinks you are perfect for each other because you are pretending to be someone you are not?

Don't do or say anything that contradicts who you are or what you believe in, just to get him to like you.

You want him to like you for who you are, not for who you are not.

Jacob and Kerri have been married now for just over a year. When they were dating the two were inseparable. They would regularly go roller blading, bike riding, to the beach, to parties, out on his motorcycle, as well as many other fun things. Jacob absolutely loved her and how active she was. Now that they are married, Kerri has backed off from doing just about everything, and most nights she just prefers to stay in. When Jacob confronted her about the situation, she told him that she was just doing all those things so she could get him to commit, and now that he is fully committed, she can just do what she wants. She also cut her hair short, is wearing much less make up, and has gained a lot of weight. She feels because Jacob is fully committed to her, that she can let herself go on top of everything else. Poor Jacob doesn't even know who he is married to anymore. He has a wife who is deceptive and dishonest. She was doing nothing but lying to him about who she really was, just so she could get a guy to commit to her. Kerri isn't happy in her marriage either because she initially pretended to be someone she's not, just to hook a man. She is being incongruent with who she really is, which causes a tremendous amount of anxiety for her. It should come as no big surprise that they are now getting divorced.

If you want to be happy with your relationship, then you have to remain true to who you are and find a guy who you are compatible with. This is what happens when you try to change yourself into something that you think HE likes, instead of just being yourself. If he doesn't like you for who you are, then too bad! Not your problem. You'll find someone better who will love you for exactly who you are.

TOPICS TO AVOID ON A DATE

Religion

If this is going to be a deal breaker for you, then it is something that you better find out before your first date. If you get half way through the date and are having a great time, but then find out you have to 'kick him to the curb' because he is not Latvian Orthodox, then you just wasted both of your time.

Politics

Differing political views can turn an otherwise perfect first date into disaster. Don't ruin things for yourself or for him by bringing this up. A political discussion is far from light! There will be plenty of time for you to discuss this in the future if it is that important to you.

Exes

This may seem obvious, but this is not the time to go into detail about your ex boyfriends, or even bring them up at all. If you do find you need to reference an ex during your date, keep it very light and non-threatening, almost like an after thought. Better yet, don't do it at all.

Marriage and kids

You can subtly ask him what he is looking for if you want, but the key here is subtle. If you can't be subtle then it is best avoiding this subject on the first date. Now is not the time to start planning your life together. Touch on the subject quickly and move on. It's just a first date remember.

Money

You would think this would be another obvious one. I once was on a date where immediately after getting into my car, the girl said to me, "So do you think you are going to be getting a better car soon?" For the record, my car at the time was a Honda Civic that was only a year old. Half way through the date she flat out asked me how much money I made. Come on! If these things really are that important to you, at least be subtle about it. Most guys are afraid of gold diggers, so if he suspects you may be one, then don't expect there to be a second date.

THE QUESTION GAME

One really fun way to find out about someone on a first date is to play the question game. This was an idea I got while on a date years ago, which I then stole from her and used it successfully on many dates in the future. It completely solves the problem of what to talk about, as it gives you lots of material and can be fun at the same time. You can start off by simply saying, "let's play the question game." He'll of course ask what the question game is, so you'll then tell him about the game and the rules. The question game is basically where you ask each other one question at a time with the following rules:

1. They have to be interesting questions. Nothing like, "what is your favorite color or do you like fruit?" SNORE!!! Always remember to be fun!
2. You can't ask the same question immediately after it was asked. If you ask him what his most embarrassing moment was, he can't come back and ask you the same question right afterwards. He can however ask it later!
3. You tell him who goes first, and this part is up to you. If you want to maintain full control, then you can go first by asking him something you would like to know.

You can start off light and easy and then get progressively more racy. Just a warning, the question game can turn quite sexual. I personally made a point of turning it sexual just to get my date thinking about sex while in my presence. It was a powerful tool, so just be careful that it doesn't lead you down the wrong path.

Some good questions to ask are as follows:

- If you could meet any historical figure, who would it be and why?
- If you could live anywhere in the world, where would it be?
- If you could have any job in the world without any chance of failure, what would it be?
- What are you most passionate about?
- What is the craziest thing you have ever done?
- If you could have a super power, what would it be and why would you want that power?
- What would you do with the money if you won the lottery?
- If your house was on fire and you could only save one material item, what would it be?
- -True or false "All is fair in love and war.'
- How many relationships have you had?
- When was the first time you had sex? (A dangerous road to go down as you are now turning it sexual. Use discretion.)

Notice how I start off with lighter questions and then gradually shift into the relationship and then finally the sex questions. If you are going to ask about sex, the game will most likely progress to being more and more sexual. This can be fun, but just be conscious of what it can lead to. It very well may be to a question from him, "Do you want to get out of here?' There is nothing wrong with turning it sexual but if you are looking for a serious relationship, you may want to avoid turning it too sexual too soon or it can send the wrong message. I'll be talking more about sex in the next chapter.

WHO SHOULD PAY?

You reach the end of your fabulous dinner at the Olive Garden when the waiter drops the check in the middle of the table. He continues talking and the check just sits there like the elephant in the room. Tradition says that the man should pay, and I do agree with this for the most part, but there is much more to it than that.

If he is leading the way and is the one who asks you out, then yes, he should pay, fairly simple. There are some that say you should at least offer to pay half the check. You can do this if you like, and I do think it is a nice gesture, but it isn't necessary on the first or second date. Don't think you are in any way obligated to him if you don't pay half. Obligated for what? It's just a date, and you don't owe him anything. If he feels you owe him something, then that's his problem and I would move on to someone else. On the third date however, go ahead and make a sincere offer to cover half of the bill. As you continue to date him you can either continue to split the check or you can alternate who pays. Continuing to let him pay throughout the relationship can throw up an unnecessary barrier that you don't need and can eventually lead to him losing interest in you. Relationships are partnerships, and your partner shouldn't be expected to continue to pay throughout the relationship. That isn't a partnership. That's gold digger territory.

Relationships are partnerships, and your partner shouldn't be expected to continue to pay throughout the relationship.

Guys are turned off by gold diggers, so you definitely want to ensure you are sending the right message. If he pays on your date, and you end up going for dessert afterwards, or have to grab a cab anywhere, then make a sincere offer to pay for these smaller things. It is a very nice gesture that we appreciate. If you aren't planning on going anywhere else after, offer to pay the tip. If he refuses and insists on paying for everything, then accept that and don't ask more than once. You offered, and he will appreciate that.

If you were the one asking him out then you should make a sincere offer to pay or expect to pay at least half of the check. It's rude to ask someone out and then expect them to pay.

Be honest and don't play ridiculous games intended to trick or deceive. You expect him to be honest with you so you should be extending him that same courtesy. I was watching a local talk show where they were talking about dating. One of the girls on the show said that she will absolutely insist on paying half for the first three dates. If the guy refuses, she offers again and said she would make a very good case for why she should pay half. If he accepts her offer at anytime during the first three dates, she cuts him loose immediately. This deceptive behavior is flat out ridiculous. She is eliminating good possible candidates for no legitimate reason. Don't discredit guys for stupid things like this. It is hard enough to meet good, quality people who you have chemistry with to begin with. You don't need added BS getting in the way of you finding Mr. Right.

WHERE TO GO ON A DATE

Men are typically expected to know where they are taking you, and to be in control of making the dating decisions. Women can be easily turned off if the guy doesn't have any ideas and just says, "whatever you want to do." Boring! There are times though where you may want to make some suggestions, or ask him out for future dates. The worst date is dinner and a movie. Blechk! Why would anyone want to see a movie knowing that you won't even be able to talk to your date? I used to do that way back when I was young and clueless. You want to keep things as interesting as possible.

Here are some great ideas for non-traditional dates:

- billiards
- rollerblading
- mini golf
- driving range
- batting cages
- swimming

- the beach
- rock climbing
- sailing
- skiing
- ice skating
- horseback riding
- hiking
- a bus tour of your own city
- art gallery or museum
- amusement or theme park
- salsa class
- improvisational comedy class

Any of the above can be really fun. Just remember to not take anything on the date too seriously! Make having fun your first priority!

Chapter Nine Highlights

✓ Never forget the main purpose of the first date. It is to establish if there is chemistry and that you will have fun together.

✓ Don't approval seek and answer questions honestly. The first date is when you form the roots of your relationship.

✓ Be honest!

- ✓ Keep conversation light
- ✓ Avoid talking about religion, politics, exes, kids/marriage and money
- ✓ Play the question game
- ✓ The guy should pay if he asked you out. You can offer to pick up the tip or if you go somewhere else such as for dessert, offer to pay. This little gesture goes a long way.

Now that we have covered everything up to the end of the first date, it is time to look at what comes next. If you like the guy, you are going to want to date him, which will hopefully lead to a commitment.

CHAPTER TEN

DATING AND COMMITMENT

"We are all a little weird and life's a little weird,
and when we find someone whose weirdness
is compatible with ours, we join up with them
and fall in mutual weirdness and call it love."
~Dr. Seuss

Now that the first date is out of the way, and assuming things went well, we now play the cat and mouse game once again as to who calls whom. If he had a good time, he will definitely get in touch with you again, so sit back and wait for him to contact you. He may call or text the next day or he may wait for a couple of days. If he takes two days or longer, don't think it means he isn't interested in you. There is a stupid, unwritten rule that guys should wait two days before calling after a date. It's a little old school, and my preference is to contact the person the next day. Some guys may still be following the old school mentality by waiting and might be dying to contact you in the interim. They discussed this in a humorous way in the movie Swingers where they said that women know about this rule and are expecting the guy to wait two days. Three days would have made it look like they were just trying to get around the two-day rule, so they settled on four days to completely throw them off. This is funny in a movie for sure, but completely ridiculous in real life.

Keep in mind that most guys really have no idea what to do here and many of them seriously over think this. They don't realize that they should be calling the next day. If he takes weeks to call you, then there really aren't too many excuses to justify that amount of time. He really isn't into you in this case so don't waste time with him.

Men who are only interested in sex know they need to keep some distance, which particularly applies to the early stages of dating. If you are only hearing from him once per week, and he seems to take forever to return your calls or texts, then he is probably just interested in sex. Don't waste your time, energy, or emotions unless you think you can find happiness through wasting your time.

KEEP YOUR OPTIONS OPEN

Rebecca had one of the best dates of her life with Jesse and two days have gone by without contact. She thinks he may be the man she has been looking for as she can't remember the last time she was this excited about one particular guy. She is having trouble focusing at work, isn't going out with her friends, and she stopped going to her dance classes. She doesn't want to miss his call. She is obsessing over him, which is a recipe for disaster and disappointment.

When you really like someone, it is only natural to think about him constantly. The biggest problem with this is that you start to become obsessed, which can lead to coming across as needy, being too available, or seeking approval from him. You may even find yourself putting off your life for this person by avoiding your friends and skipping out on things that you normally enjoy doing, just so you can be more available for him. All of this can be very unhealthy when trying to form a relationship as it sabotages your ability to think and be your regular, fun self. You run the risk of being taken advantage of. Men who are particularly good with women can sense this approval seeking behavior like a shark smelling blood in the water, or a cheetah sensing a wounded gazelle (Can you tell I watch Animal Planet?) This can lead to you being taken advantage of, and/or the guy losing complete respect for you.

The Law of Attraction states that whatever you think about most becomes your reality. While this may be true to an extent, it doesn't apply when you are obsessing over a man. The reason is that obsession can lead to negative thoughts and images of things not going well. This in turn, can divert energy to negative thoughts instead of positive, thereby attracting what you don't want. So how can you avoid obsessing so much over one guy?

You need to have options.

Having options means dating multiple men at the same time. Note, dating multiple men does not mean you are sleeping with multiple men. This is especially important if you are looking for a serious relationship. Not just so you don't obsess over one particular guy, but also to help ensure you find the right person. By having options, you will be far less likely to seek approval on your dates, and may actually end up having more fun on them. You aren't putting all your eggs in one basket, which will make it far easier to avoid obsessing.

Don't start looking at any one guy as anything serious just yet, regardless of how much fun you had with him on your date. You don't know that much about him yet, so why would you give him an exclusive designation? That is something he has to earn with you. Take your mind off of him by meeting as many men as possible, and group the dates closely together. When I say closely together, I mean in the same week, not in the same day. Once I walked a girl home after my date with her and her next date was waiting for her in the car out front of her building. Awkward!

If you want a serious relationship that could possibly lead to marriage, why on earth would you not want to have more than one choice?

If you were shopping for a wedding dress, are you going to buy the first one you try on because you think it 'isn't bad?' Or are you going to try on multiple dresses to find the one that is perfect for you? The same logic applies to dating.

Sometimes you don't truly know what you want until you find it. The rest of your life and your happiness depend on it. Take your time, have fun, and improve your odds on making the right choice.

Having options may also remove some of the pressure or performance anxiety you may feel if you meet someone you really like. The more you like a guy, the more nervous you may become. You start to put added pressure on yourself, which may cause you to clam up and possibly come across as boring or uninteresting during your date. This situation worsens when you don't have any other options at the time. If this is the only guy you are talking to, then you don't have any other dates lined up if this one doesn't work out as well as you hoped. By having more men available to you, you have options, which can remove a tremendous amount of nervousness.

Let's say for example you are selected to participate in a contest where you can win $100,000 if you can sink a basketball from the three-point line. How would you feel if you only had one chance to make the shot to win the $100,000 compared to if you had ten chances? You are still of course going to try on each shot, but there won't be anywhere near as much pressure on you to successfully make it. Your breathing will be slower and calmer and you will be able to think and focus more clearly, thereby improving your chances on each and every shot you make. It is exactly the same with dating. If you have a few guys that you like lined up, you will find it far easier to be your true, interesting and fun self than if you only have the one shot.

SEX

In the early stages of a relationship, women have a tremendous amount of power over men, even if it may not seem that way. Once a woman has sex, she loses this power. This is one of the reasons why it is so important for you to be clear about what you are looking for. If you aren't looking for anything too serious, then by all means, have a good time. You can have sex on the first date if you choose. It really isn't that big of a deal to most men. Unlike most women, men can easily have sex without any sort of emotional attachment. In fact, to many men, sex isn't any more meaningful than shaking hands. Don't ever think that sleeping with a man is going to make him like you more or get him to commit. It never will. Ever. That kind of thinking is only going to get you hurt.

Don't ever think that sleeping with a man is going to make him like you more or get him to commit.

Most guys will generally try to have sex with you as soon as they possibly can. Before I met Kelly, there were times when I would have sex not just on my first date, but that WAS the first date! We don't need to know your name. We don't need to know anything about you. All we need to know is that we are physically attracted to you and that's good enough for us! It's unfortunate that this is the way we are, but this is the truth. We have evolutionary programming to ensure survival of the species, and this is exactly why we have this attitude towards sex.

By having sex too quickly, you could be indirectly sabotaging the relationship before it even gets started. You have this power, so you should use it. It will drive him nuts, (in a good way). He may constantly try to sleep with you, so you will need lots of willpower. If you don't have the willpower, you will succumb. I can't tell you how many times I have been with a girl when she said, "I never thought we would be doing that tonight." The funny thing is that I had a pretty good idea it would be happening, and that was before I even invited any of them out.

Many women will say the best time to have sex is when it feels right and for many, this 'feeling right' comes after three dates in their mind. I have found this translates into about six to eight hours of time. This is regardless of whether the time is spent all on the first meeting, first date or over five dates. If I have more than eight hours invested in a woman, and she has still not slept with me, then it definitely gets my attention. It makes her different from all the rest. If I was just looking to have sex with her and nothing else, then I would stop pursuing her. By waiting a little longer, she just saved herself from having sex with someone who wasn't serious about her. On the other hand, if I really liked her and I was looking for something more serious, I would continue dating and courting her.

Rules on when to have sex

There is no hard rule with when to sleep with someone, so don't implement one. Three dates? Really? Who says so? Many men, including myself know that most women feel comfortable sleeping with someone after the third date. If a guy suggests coming over to his place to 'watch a movie' on the third date, then he is probably planning on having sex with you. 'Watch a movie' is code for having sex. If he says he just wants to cuddle, you can bet on the fact that he is going to try for more. It can be very easy for a confident man to seduce you from this point, even if you weren't expecting or planning on it to happen. Men expect some resistance during sexual escalation for the first time, so don't be afraid to resist in order to slow things down. Men who are particularly good with women know that if they do encounter resistance, it may just be token resistance. While women may deep down want to proceed, they don't want to feel as though they are giving it up to easily. Players know that if they get serious resistance, they can create a 'state break', where they change the overall mood entirely. A state is just another way to describe the way you feel. A state break is a sudden change in the way you feel. If you are happy, your state is happiness. In this case, your state is sexual pleasure. You are enjoying it, so a state break would interrupt this good feeling. He may say something like, 'yes, you are right, let's stop'. He'll then turn on the lights and turn off the music to change her state. She liked the feelings she was just having before, and now he has taken them away. He will try again in about five or ten minutes and knows that there is a good chance he won't encounter the same resistance again. Be conscious of this behavior.

Okay, so when can you have sex?

I thought you might ask that. When you actually have sex depends on how frequently you see him. If he is making an effort to only see you once a week, then all that much more reason why you should wait longer, as that could mean sex is all he is after. You need to find out for sure. If a guy is only looking for sex, it is unlikely he is going to let it go more than three dates. If he hasn't gotten sex by the third date, then that is the last you will see of him. Good riddance. You just saved yourself from sleeping with someone who wasn't serious about you from the start. To test to see if a guy is truly interested in a relationship, hold off on having sex for a bit longer. I would say no earlier than the fifth date, but if you can extend it even a little longer, then you can feel all that more confident in his intentions. Don't let your emotions misguide you here. Someone who is really good with women can press the right buttons to make you feel very comfortable, especially after eight hours of comfort building. Even if you feel like it is the right time, always give it that extra bit of time to be sure. You could wait an extra week or so to improve the chances of a relationship forming, or you could have sex with him early and jeopardize the whole thing. This is a powerful technique, so use it to your advantage. It is your power. As long as the guy feels like he is progressing, and he likes you, then he isn't going to lose interest.

The key here is that things need to be progressing. I once went on four dates with a girl I legitimately liked, but she wouldn't even make out with me (I can't even imagine how any woman could resist!) Going four dates without even making out makes me think that she was frigid, or had her own personal issues. Whatever they were, it was up to her to sort out, but she would have to do that without me, as I was no longer interested. I'm interested in being intimate and progressing in my relationships, not to mention having strong communication. I tried to ask her about it, but she wouldn't open up to me even slightly. I gave her a solid shot, but no go. I was out of there.

Don't think you can wait five dates? On the first date you can hint to him that you like to really get to know someone before having sex and that you prefer to take things slow. This is something that can work if you have strong chemistry and are having a great time with him. If he really likes you, then he won't make a big deal about it. If he does, then it is possible that his intentions are not in line with yours. If he is okay waiting, then you can always surprise him with sex a little earlier if you feel comfortable with it. Just be sure to use this at your discretion and if there are any doubts at all, then you are better off waiting a little longer.

YOU ARE THE BOSS...ALWAYS

You are always in control and never forget it. Men like to feel like they are in control and many women prefer a man who has this covered. It shows her that he can take care of her and his family. This goes back to evolutionary programming where the man is the provider for the family. Being a provider is something that men need to do to feel like men. We need to be providing for you and it is our duty to make you happy. After all, if you are not happy, we know damn well you will make sure we are not happy! This is what gives you so much power.

Being a provider is something that men need to do to feel like men. We need to be providing for you and it is our duty to make you happy.

I used to do pricing estimates for a painting company and ninety-nine percent of the time, it was the woman who picked the color. The men knew that they would never hear the end of it if they picked the wrong color, or even influenced her decision on picking the wrong color. This doesn't just apply to choosing colors, but to almost everything in the relationship. We want to make you happy and look at it as our duty to make you happy, and when you are happy, we are happy! Happy?

Don't confuse being in control with being controlling. No one likes someone who is controlling, and if you see signs of anything resembling controlling behavior, then you need to bail on the relationship fast. Again, you are always in control and always the boss. If you are in a relationship with someone who is controlling or have been in the past it is only because at some point you gave him control. You handed him the reins. I assure you, when you first met, you were the boss and in full control, regardless of how assertive he may have been.

DESPERATE AND NEEDY

We all have 'needs.' We need food, we need shelter, we need money, just as we need to be touched and we need to be loved. Don't be afraid of having needs. Be afraid of being needy. Nothing will scare a guy off faster than coming across as being needy.

What are some examples of needy behavior?

- Any excessive calling, emailing or texting him
- Constantly asking him how he feels about you
- Constantly telling him how you feel about him hoping he will give you reassurance in return
- Asking him if he thinks you are good enough for him

- Always demanding to know his whereabouts
- Constantly seeking his approval on just about everything you do
- Getting upset every time you don't get your own way
- Flipping out every time he doesn't text you back immediately

I can't even begin to tell you how unattractive neediness is. Just as women have a strong intuition with most things, men have a strong intuition for picking up on neediness, and as soon as we do, you are one foot out the door. You don't want to be spending your Friday nights sitting on your couch by yourself watching re-runs of Desperate Housewives, do you?

While you should never feel that you 'need a man' to make you happy, you shouldn't be uttering such comments either. By saying things like "I don't need a man", you are putting this negativity out into the universe, and it responds by keeping you single. It can also lead to misandry, which would lead to men wanting nothing to do with you at all.

DO YOU ASSUME HE WANTS THE SAME THING?

So many women will start dating someone thinking that just because they want a relationship, then he must as well. Based on that assumption, they continue dating the guy they think is their man. Bad idea. A woman can quite literally waste years with one guy based on this assumption. You can't assume he is looking for a relationship, unless he has specifically said he is looking for one with you. The 'with you' part is important as he can easily say he is looking for a relationship without meaning he is interested in a relationship with you, and he wouldn't necessarily be lying. He may very well want a relationship, just not with you, so make sure that is clear and don't assume anything. Are you in a relationship right now?

Take a moment to answer yes or no to the following questions to determine if you are in a relationship or not. If you think the comment means you are in a relationship then write YES, and if it doesn't then write NO.

- He introduced me to his parents
- It has been three months and we talk every single day
- We are going on a two-week vacation to the Bahamas
- We see each other every day
- We see each other at least once a week and it has been a year
- We have been on 10 dates
- We have been on 20 dates

Did you answer yes to any of the questions? Your answer should have been no for every single one. If you indicated yes, then you are making assumptions, regardless of how logical those assumptions may be to you.

Don't just arbitrarily assume you are in a relationship! Determining if you are in a relationship takes clear and concise communication, not assumptions. Your relationship status is something that needs to be discussed. Unless he is specifically referring to you as his girlfriend, then he most likely doesn't view your situation as a relationship. This doesn't mean you should start referring to him as your boyfriend all of a sudden though, as it can imply neediness.

DEFINING THE RELATIONSHIP

There will come a time when you will have to find out where your relationship is heading, or if you even have one at all. There is a time and a place for this discussion, and it is important that it is done correctly in order to keep awkwardness to a minimum. Never try to press for a relationship too soon, or he may withdraw. You don't want to push him into something serious with you before he even has a chance to realize that you are what he wants. If a couple of months go by and he hasn't started to escalate things with you then it is a fair assumption that he is still playing the field. Some guys can keep this charade going on for years (I know, I did it myself). You can only let this go on for so long before you need to find out how he feels. There is of course a right way and a wrong way to approach the situation. You don't want to push him into anything he doesn't want, as this decision has to be mutual and without feeling any unnecessary pressure. You also don't want to come across as needy or pushy in any way.

Don't start talking with him about where things are going, or bring up relationships. Instead, pull back a little and let him give chase. The fear of losing you may be enough to trigger him into committing. You can even go so far as to say that you want some space for yourself, as you are not sure if this is what you really want. If he is truly serious about you then he will bite. If he isn't then you will find that out as well. This is where it is crucial for you to be impartial either way. It may kill you inside, as you don't want to lose him, but ask yourself this... what do you really 'have' with him right now?

Wouldn't you rather **know right now** that he likes you as much as you like him? Or would you prefer to waste another year of your life?

If you still feel the need to discuss it then there is definitely a time and a place to bring this up. I find that many women will bring this up at the strangest times, which makes the conversation all that much more awkward and uncomfortable.

- On the drive out of town for a camping trip the Friday afternoon before the Labor Day long weekend is NOT the time to bring it up.
- On the drive over to have Easter dinner with your family is NOT the time to bring it up.
- At the airport waiting to catch the flight leaving for your two-week vacation to the Bahamas is NOT the time to bring it up.
- At any time while on the above vacation is NOT the time to bring it up.

Are you seeing a pattern here? Anytime where the two of your are going to be trapped together for any duration of time, or even on your way to do something together is not a good time to bring this up, or any other important conversation or 'talk' for that matter. A crowded coffee shop, restaurant or night club are also bad ideas for this conversation. Good times to bring it up might be once you get back from the camping trip you took on the long weekend, or better yet, a couple of days after the trip. Come over to his home on a weekday evening or have him come over to your place. Discuss it in a quiet place where you can both think clearly. If you try to have the conversation where he is trapped with you, then you may not get an honest answer, or you may push him to give an answer that he is not sure about, which may only set you up for disappointment later. It is also possible that he will try to evade the question all together. It can be hard enough to bring up something like this as it is, so don't do it at a time where he is likely going to evade the question, forcing you to bring it up at another time. I have dated some women who would bring it up, only for me to conveniently evade the question, and then they would never bring it up again. I was happy about that, but it wasn't a good situation for them.

Another bad time to bring it up would be after you have been making out with him on the couch for the past thirty minutes and are starting to strip each others clothes off like you are peeling bananas. One of the worst times to ask! I remember dating one girl who apparently thought this was the perfect time! NO! If you want a commitment before moving forward with sex, then that doesn't mean squeezing it out of him immediately before moving forward with sex! In that situation you just need to tell him you would rather wait. If he likes you, he will respect that. You don't want to be discussing something serious when both of you have hormones flaring. You could easily end up with a guy telling you just what you want to hear. Since he feels like he is very close to having sex, it would be easy for him to just say, "sure, whatever." Afterwards, he will be questioning himself on why he just committed to you causing him to feel buyer's remorse, which will set the relationship up for failure very fast.

So what is the best way to go about defining the relationship so you know exactly where you stand?

You want to let him know that he can take some time to think about it if needed. You want to take the pressure off to ensure he makes the right decision. Remember, this is not all about YOU. Don't be selfish! It is about both of you together.

There is no 'easy' way to do this, and there is no doubt it can be scary. After all, you like this guy and you are really hoping he feels the same way you do. It can be easy to put this off for fear of a negative response, but putting it off is the last thing you should do. Just how much time do you have to waste? As I mentioned earlier, it can be years before you find out his true intentions unless you step up to the plate and face the fire now. If he is on the same page as you and wants to be in a relationship with you, then his response will be positive. If he doesn't, then his response will be negative, and although this is not what you want, wouldn't you rather know about it now?

When to define the relationship

We've talked about the logistics of *where* to define the relationship, but *when* in the dating phase do you define it? There really is no 'perfect' time. If you jump on this too early, then there is a good chance you will scare him away. I would say it really depends on how often you see him. If you see him every single day, then you may want to consider it after six to eight weeks. If you see each other less frequently, then I wouldn't bring anything up before three months. If it has been three months and you get a negative response, then I wouldn't necessarily bail just yet, but it is definitely time to start pulling away. If he starts to give chase, then use that power to your advantage, as you now know that he is in fact interested in you. Give it no more than a few more weeks and then you can bring it up again. If he still won't commit then kick him to the curb. He isn't what you are looking for. Don't waste your time.

What to say

Just as there is no perfect time for defining the relationship, there is also no perfect thing to say, just don't say, "We have to talk." Ooooohhhh... men HATE this! It has such a negative connotation to it that it puts men on the defensive immediately. This concept doesn't just apply when defining the relationship, but it applies throughout your entire relationship, including when you are married, and right through until the day they close the lid.

So what do you say? Whatever you do, just don't start pouring your heart out in a river of emotion hoping he is going to feel the same as you. This will only come across as needy and have the opposite effect than what you hoped for. You are best starting off with statements as opposed to questions. Statements are far less invasive and non-threatening; in other words, you will be less stressed out this way. You can try saying something like "I really enjoy spending time with you and really don't care to see other people anymore." Then stop and wait for his reply. Regardless of what his answer is, don't get mad or defensive. It is what it is and now you know for sure. If he says he doesn't want to be in a serious relationship, then he doesn't. It still is possible that he may, but just not with you. Take what he says word for word and stop trying to find the hidden meaning behind it. There isn't one. Take it for what it is and move on. Stop overanalyzing. He isn't for you.

DISCOVER YOUR DEAL BREAKERS

Daryl and Diana seem like the perfect couple. They do everything together and are practically inseparable. They finish each other's sentences and have many of the same interests. About four months into their relationship, they found themselves on the discussion of kids and it turns out that Daryl is not a big fan of the little rug rats. In fact, he doesn't like or want kids at all. It has always been Diana's dream to fall in love, get married and have kids one day. Now she is finding out that this will never happen if she stays with Daryl. All this time building a connection with someone who has just introduced a deal breaker for her. This is why it is so important to determine if there are any deal breakers now before getting too far into a relationship (as you did in the exercises in Chapter Three).

GIVING SPACE

Sometimes men need a little bit of room to breathe. If you crowd a guy too much, you can scare him off, so it is better to have too much space than not enough. You may want to see him every day, but if you are always there, then he may start to back off a bit. Sometimes guys need to have some time for themselves, so the last thing you want to do is smother them. This includes texting and calling. If you are always the one initiating the texts or phone calls, or if you text or call too frequently then I assure you this will scare him away. Do you remember the story about Rhonda? The girl I dated who always felt she needed to get in the last text? It was annoying and made me think that she may have some issues. It's okay if he is the last one to text. Don't feel you always need to have the last word.

If he says he is going to have a guys night out on Saturday night, tell him to have fun and don't make a big deal over it. You should be having regular nights out with the girls as well. This is especially important if you are seeing each other frequently. Sometimes you need to take a bit of time apart just so you can miss each other a little.

Make sure you give him some space… or he will give you LOTS of space if you know what I mean.

DOES YOUR MAN LOOK AT OTHER WOMEN?

I recently did an online survey where I asked women for some reasons as to why they would reject a guy after they have already established mutual attraction. The number one answer was that he was looking at other girls (71% of women).

Lori and Jason had just started dating and were out a grocery store picking up a few things for a dinner they were going to cook together that evening. They were walking down the produce isle when Jason noticed a package containing some interesting looking fruit. He picked it up for closer inspection at which point Lori came over to find out what he was looking at. "You really find those pumpkins interesting, don't you?" she remarked. "Oh, that's what they are! I was trying to figure it out as I haven't seen anything like this in a grocery store before" he replied. Lori went completely quiet. In fact, she was quiet for the rest of the day, into the evening and through the night. It wasn't until the early hours of the morning that she broke her silence. "So you really found those pumpkins interesting this afternoon." Jason couldn't believe she was still thinking about that! "Why are you so concerned that I was looking at some pumpkins? Do you think I was looking at them to avoid looking at another girl in the store or something?"

"Well…I didn't say that, but if that is what you are saying, then that must be the case" she said quietly.

In the true story above, Jason really was just interested in figuring out what the mystery fruit was. While there may have been another girl present at the time, in this particular case, he didn't notice her. Even if he did, there is looking and there is gawking. Men are always going to notice other women. Always. That is something that you are going to have to accept regardless of who you are dating. It doesn't mean that we aren't interested in you, think any less of you or are comparing you to her. As men, we look at women we find attractive. It is in our blood. It is what we do, and always will do. It doesn't matter who the guy is. He could be the teenager working the drive thru window at McDonald's or he could be the leader of a G7 country -and everyone in between. Even if you don't think your guy checks out other women, trust me he does. We look because it is in our programming. Don't take it personally! Most of the time, it is harmless. Now, if he is gawking, turning his head at everything in a skirt, and making comments then you may want to consider kicking him to the curb.

SHOULD YOU CHANGE FOR HIM?

Let's say that you met a guy who you knew really liked you. Although he knew that you liked dark haired men that dressed with more of a rock n' roll edge, yet he had blonde hair and dressed preppy. One day, he shows up with his hair dyed black and dressed like he just came out of a Mötley Crüe video, just so he can improve his chances of getting you to like him. Would you respect him? No need to answer as I already know what you are thinking. You really wouldn't have much respect for him as he is trying to be someone that he is not. So should you make changes in your life to make him like you more?

Absolutely not!

Just as you wouldn't respect a guy if he made all kinds of changes in his life just to 'get you', don't do that for him either, as he won't respect you. The reasoning for this goes beyond a relationship with the guy you are dating. If you are not happy with who you are, then by all means make changes. But any changes you make have to be for *you*, and not for anyone else. If you continue trying to change to please others then you also won't be happy in other areas of your life. You have to remain true to your own identity. This is not just about changing yourself to make him like you more, it is about altering your life in order to better fit into his.

If on a weekly basis you normally play in a soccer league, meet up with your friends, and go to the gym, then you need to continue doing these things, as these are the things that you enjoy doing. They make you happy. If all of a sudden you find that you are skipping the gym, soccer and are alienating your friends so you can spend more time with a particular guy, then you are changing for him. So what do you think is going to happen? While it might seem good in the beginning, your happiness level is going to start declining, because you changed your life for someone and are no longer being true to who *you* are, or doing what *you* want to do. This change in lifestyle will end up showing through on the exterior as well, which he will pick up on. Because you changed, you are no longer the woman your man was originally attracted to. You have changed and may now very well be coming across as needy. This leads to the demise of the relationship.

Never be afraid of losing the guy just because he doesn't like your lifestyle! It's who you are and you are doing what you enjoy. Always love yourself and put yourself first. Again, if you can't be in love with yourself the way you are, then how can you expect anyone else to love you? This applies to all relationships in your life.

QUID PRO QUO

I have seen many women do just about whatever they have to in order to please their men. They will buy surprise gifts, clean his apartment, tidy and organize his closet, give hour-long massages and much more. They sometimes will do these things for very little in return. It is great to do nice things for your guy, but you should be getting the same treatment in return. You are looking for a partner in life, therefore he should act as one. As men, we really want to please you, and this means doing things for you as well. You want him to view you as an equal, his second half, not as a servant. You shouldn't be doing anymore for him than he is for you. The deal should be 50/50, give and take. Quid pro quo. He will respect you more for it in the end. By continuing to do nice things for him with nothing in return, you may start to develop resentment, which is an extremely negative emotion. This resentment will lead to changes in your behavior around him, which will change the energy flow in the relationship from positive to negative. He will pick up on the difference, which can send the relationship downhill from there.

This is something that needs to be established right at the beginning of the relationship. If he gets used you doing all these nice things for him and then you start pulling back, he may start to question why. Don't get him used to something only to take it away. Start it early on and form a healthy relationship from the beginning. Don't let him walk all over you and he will respect you more for it. If he needs some encouragement to help you out with anything, then just ask! Often, that is all it takes.

Chapter Ten Highlights

- ✓ Don't attach too much meaning to when a guy calls or texts after a first date. However, if he takes a week then he most likely isn't looking for anything serious with you.
- ✓ Have options by dating multiple men at a time. This doesn't mean sleeping with multiple men.
- ✓ Women attach more meaning to sex than men do. Men can easily separate sex from emotion.
- ✓ Don't have sex before five dates to test his seriousness.
- ✓ Men will push for sex with you at their first opportunity.
- ✓ Men are okay waiting for sex as long as they see a natural progression.
- ✓ You are the boss. Now, and always.
- ✓ Never say things like 'I don't need a man' as this is the negative message you are sending out into the universe. The universe will then answer by keeping you single.
- ✓ Never assume he wants the same thing as you.
- ✓ Don't try to jump into a relationship too soon.
- ✓ The best way to define a relationship is to pull back and let him give chase. He will if he doesn't want to lose you.
- ✓ Never just assume the guy you are dating wants the same thing you do. The only way to know you are in a committed relationship is to discuss it with him.
- ✓ Never have a discussion to define the relationship at a time when both of you are trapped together for any duration of time.

- ✓ Defining the relationship is NOT about you. It is about both of you together as a couple. Don't be selfish!
- ✓ Be sure to give him enough space
- ✓ Never change your lifestyle to please a man
- ✓ Never be afraid of losing him while following anyone of these guidelines.
- ✓ There should be a 50/50 give and take. Quid pro quo.

There is no doubt a lot of psychology around building a successful relationship. It can however be far easier if you are coming from a solid place within. It's now time to discuss finding true happiness throughout the entire dating sequence.

CHAPTER ELEVEN

YOUR QUEST FOR HAPPINESS

"Most folks are as happy
as they make up their minds to be."
~ Abraham Lincoln

I find that a lot of people could be happier than they are right now. Really, you, and only you, can decide on how happy you want to be. I know, easier said than done, but the only thing really keeping you from true happiness is your mind. When you are happier, you naturally draw more happy and positive people into your life and this could definitely include Mr. Right. Do you think that he is going to recognize you as the woman of his dreams if you are walking around looking like Miss Grumpy Pants every day? Highly unlikely! The same would apply if a guy approached you who is apparently down on himself with a big frown on his face. You aren't going to give him the time of day! Even though this may not be who you really are, you are demonstrating to the world that this is who you are. You are lying to them by keeping all your inner beauty tied up inside. You are not only ripping yourself off by depriving yourself of happiness, but you are ripping the world off of all the gifts you have to offer, and this includes Mr. Right.

You are not only ripping yourself off by depriving yourself of happiness, but you are ripping the world off of all the gifts you have to offer, and this includes Mr. Right.

Take a moment right now and think about the three most important people in your life. Do you have them? Great. It is always helpful to have other positive people around you, as you will absorb their energy, which in turn makes it easier for you to be happy for no reason. Really, you can be happy for no reason if you simply just *choose* to be happy. From your list of the three most important people in your life, who was number one? Was it you? I truly hope it was, but something tells me that it wasn't.

Happiness, and self-confidence begin with your self-esteem. How you feel about yourself. How do you expect anyone else to love you if you don't love yourself? How can you give love to other people when you don't love yourself? On commercial flights, they always ask for you to secure your own oxygen mask first, before helping anyone else. It doesn't matter if it is your child, your mother, your brother, or your friend. You have to take care of yourself first. After all, if you aren't around, then who is going to take care of your children?

When you are happy, you feel better about yourself over all. You have more self-confidence and you don't care so much about what others think of you. You become much more aware of your current surroundings, and you start to notice all the beautiful things around you.

People always seem to be running from happiness, and often it can be because we take far too many things far too seriously. Maybe if we were to all relax a little bit, and stop taking everything as seriously as we do, we all just might find this thing called happiness. There are a lot of awful things happening in the world and when we compare them with our own experiences, and our own lives, we have it pretty darn good for the most part. Regardless of how bad things may seem sometimes, there are always people worse off than you.

THE PAST

Some of us have had some pretty crappy things happen to us in the past. As unfortunate some of these things may be, it is important to realize that they are in fact in the past. There is nothing you can do to change them. What ever it may be, it happened and now it is over. The past no longer exists, so don't bring it with you into the present, and most importantly, don't bring it up with your dates! Constantly focusing on anything that has happened in the past is a complete waste of mental energy. The last thing your date wants to hear is stories about your troubled past! Again, he isn't your therapist and bringing up a troubled past is only a good idea if you want to drive him away.

When you dwell on events from the past, you are taking those problems and all the emotion that went along with them, and bringing them back into your life in the present. Let me ask you this, if you saw a movie that you didn't like, would you continue to watch it again over and over? Of course you wouldn't! But that is exactly what you are doing when you continue to dwell on your past. Every time you think about someone who may have wronged you in the past, you are re-living the emotion over and over again, and each time your mind registers this as if it happened again. You are visualizing a negative scenario. Is this really how you want to use the law of attraction? The more you think about something, the more of it you attract into your life. If you think about crap, you are going to get crap. If an ex hurt you in the past and you continue to focus on it, then guess what? He wins. You don't want him to win! You don't want him to have any satisfaction at all! You know how to get even? Forget about him and start living a happy life.

If you find that you have always dated the wrong kind of guy in the past, then the future will be no different unless you make some changes to your thinking patterns. What was real for you in the past is not real in the present, so don't make it real if it isn't. The exercises in Chapter Three will help you make the changes needed to start dating the guy you truly want… and deserve to be with.

Past mistakes aren't mistakes. They are learning experiences and that is how you must view them. I personally don't think I have made any 'mistakes' in my past. I have plenty of learning experiences though and I use them to make me a better person today. Learn from your past experiences and only hold on to the emotions that serve you. This will do wonders for your happiness.

By letting go of past baggage, it opens the door to view your future in a positive light. The future is not yet set and changing it begins with your thinking, now, in the present, TODAY.

"Everything can be taken from a man or a woman but one thing: the last of human freedoms to choose one's attitude in any given set of circumstances, to choose one's own way."
~Viktor Frankl

When you are focused on bad circumstances from your past, it makes it extremely challenging to love yourself, and that makes it harder for others to love you. These events, regardless of what they are, have already happened and there is nothing you can do to change them. They are in fact over and they no longer exist. Even if there were things you could have done differently in the past that would have made a positive difference on the outcome, what is done is done. You can't change that, but you can change the NOW which will have a positive impact on what happens to you in the future.

The same logic applies when we are wishing for a better future and always focusing on how things will one day be better than they are today. But the problem is the future does not exist! It isn't set. But do you know when it starts? It starts with the only time that *does* exist, and that time is *now*. Want to have a crystal ball and look at your future? Take a look at your past. The future will most likely be a mirror image of your past, and unless you change it, that will be your future as well. Have you always dated the same kind of guy in the past and you are not happy with it? Then things have to change, and that starts now.

The future will most likely be a mirror image of your past, and unless you change it, that will be your future as well

You need to realize that your mind is not you. It is a separate entity that doesn't define you and won't define you unless you let it. Your mind has a completely separate agenda than you do. It could be telling you a number of things: I'm not attractive enough, I'm too thin, I'm too fat, I'm too this, I'm too that. It doesn't matter what you are right now. You have to love yourself for who you are. If you don't think you are attractive enough, then there are things you can do to make yourself feel more attractive as I mentioned in Chapter Three. If you are overweight and unhappy about it, then do something about it. Exercise can really suck at the beginning, but once you start seeing some results, you will be happy you made the effort. I can't even imagine going through a week without getting my workout in each morning. For me, the pain comes from not exercising!

WORRY

"Will he call? Does he like me? Why hasn't he texted? What if he is not the one and I'm wasting my time?" Stop over analyzing everything. When you are worrying, your mind is in the future and just like with fear, worry is the anticipation of a negative outcome.

"Worrying is like a rocking chair. It will give you something to do, but it won't get you anywhere."
~Ryan Reynolds in Van Wilder

Worrying accomplishes absolutely nothing. It isn't going to have any effect on the outcome. It is just that voice in your head again telling you negative things to create the worry. By worrying all the time, you are engaging in self-sabotage. Most of the things you worry about never even actually end up happening, so why are you spending so much energy worrying about things that don't exist outside of your imagination? The best way to combat worry is to stop worrying! How do you do this you ask? According to Dale Carnegie in his book *'How to Stop Worrying and Start Living'*, there are three steps:

1. Ask yourself what is the worst thing that could ever happen in the situation you are worried about. Maybe you don't hear from him, or maybe he breaks up with you. Come to terms with the fact that this is a possibility.

2. Accept that this is a possible outcome. Understand that there are TONS of men out there and TONS of good men. Ask yourself what makes this guy so special anyway? Does he deserve you in the first place?

3. Now that you have accepted the worst, focus on how you can improve on the situations. Maybe he wasn't really the one for you anyway and now you have the opportunity to find the real Mr. Right. The one who will love you as much as you love him.

Worrying makes it almost impossible to maintain focus, not just on the guy you are worrying about, but in other areas of your life as well. Realize that when you are worrying you are not in the present moment. You are in the future, and the future does not yet exist.

"I've had a lot of worries in my life,
most of which never happened."
~ Mark Twain

BEING PRESENT

So many times we are either living in the past or living in the future. The problem with this is that it robs us of the only moment that really exists and that moment is NOW. We may think about the people who have hurt us in the past and then dwell on our negative experiences, playing them over and over again. Our subconscious mind recognizes this as the event happening over and over again which in turn has serious effects on our self-confidence and self-esteem. By focusing and replaying negative experiences from the past, you are bringing all the crappy feelings you had back then into the present moment. Don't bring crap from a time that no longer exists into the only time that does exist and the only time that matters!

As the present moment is all that you have, this is what you have to work with. Act as if you have chosen your life just as it is right now. Don't resist it. Accept it, and be thankful for everything you have now. Once you have accepted it, you are then coming from a much better place to make changes. You can't change the way your life is at the moment, but you can change the way you look at it and that is the first step to changing your life in the future.

You may have that annoying little voice in your head always telling you negative crap. When the voice is running rampant, you are daydreaming which means you are not present. How can you be present when you are busy having a conversation with yourself? You need to become conscious of it and then tell it to shut the f&%k up! It is just anxiety creating noise that needs to be silenced.

I can still remember back quite some time ago when I was out at a bar with some friends. There was one group of girls I approached that night that I still remember to this day. I wasn't very confident in approaching at the time and I was overly focused on what I was going to say next. I wasn't even *close* to being present. In fact, I was so focused on the conversation I was having in my head that I totally missed a girl telling me that she really liked me. I guess I was doing a pretty good job, but it wasn't me because I wasn't present. My response to her was, "Well, it was nice meeting you." WHAT??? Here she told me that she really liked me and I didn't even hear it. It wasn't until the next day when I was playing the interaction back in my mind when I realized what I had missed. How many others did I miss in the past when I was so busy stuck in my own head?

FEAR

When you are fearful, you are not being present. Just as with worry, fear is the anticipation of a negative outcome. Anticipation. How can you be present when you are focused on something that hasn't even happened yet and probably will not happen?

You can't feel fear in the present moment, unless maybe you are currently being chased by a hungry grizzly bear. However, that isn't the type of fear I am talking about. A grizzly bear chasing you is a very real fear, as you know that your survival is in danger. I'm talking more about a psychological fear, a fear that you fabricate in your mind without having any real evidence to support it. No grizzly bear in sight. I am referring to a fear of being alone, being rejected, looking foolish, or of what others think of you. Since you can't feel fear in the present moment, your mind becomes much clearer. You become present and will naturally draw people toward you. You are happier, your true awesomeness starts to come out and other people see it. They can sense it and it draws them to you, and this includes Mr. Right!

Some people are so busy focusing on the negative that so much of the beauty surrounding them goes unnoticed. If you are particularly negative you might be thinking, "What beauty?" It's everywhere. Look at all the great things around you and all the conveniences you have in your life. You most likely have hot and cold running water, a shower, a toilet in your home, food available to you at the grocery store that you can buy, doctors to help you when you are sick, smart phones, the internet, and a roof over your head. You may have family and friends who love you and are always there for you. What about the sky, trees, animals, children, lakes, rivers and oceans? There are millions of things around you that you can love! Just clear your mind and start taking notice. Don't wait to start. The time to start is now!

THE THREE KILLER R'S

Resentment

I talked earlier about how important it is for a relationship to be 100% give and take. If you find that you are constantly giving and receiving nothing in return, this may cause you to resent your partner. You may also have exes who have treated you badly in other ways that you are still resentful towards. By holding on to resentment, you are holding on to negative emotion from the past and you are carrying all that crap with you in the present. Hasn't your ex caused you enough grief? Leave it in the past and stop continuing to let him torment you like this. It's over.

Regret

We have all made mistakes in our lives and maybe there are some times that we would like to have back. You may regret certain things you have done or things that you didn't do. I am sure you have had at least one relationship that you have regretted. Don't fall into the trap of regretting. Just like worry or resentment, it isn't going to get you anywhere. Instead of regretting past relationships, look at what you learned from them and how they have made you a better person. By framing these regrets in a positive light, you create more positive energy that can be applied to future relationships, and the future relationships are all that matter (or your current relationship if in a good one right now).

Reacting

Have you ever found yourself in a situation where you said something to someone and the person took it as a personal attack when it wasn't intended as such? Sometimes we may think people are being critical of us when they are not. On the other hand, sometimes people really are being critical of you. You can easily control this situation by staying in control and controlling your reaction. When you have a negative reaction, you are on the defensive, which creates a huge amount of negative energy inside you. By controlling the way you react, you can control the way others react to you. If you react with anger, you will most likely get anger in return. If you react with calmness, you will get calmness in return. People tend to mirror the reaction they get, so use this to your advantage. By reacting negatively, you are exposing a weakness and creating a worse situation. Be conscious of your reactions to people and everyday situations. Be aware of the power of perception and make sure you look at things in ways that serve you and not ways that will hinder your progress.

I CAN HANDLE IT!

Sometimes life sucks and I will be the first to admit that. I remember a time when I couldn't even afford to pay rent and had to wash trucks overnight in the middle of the

Canadian winter just to make ends meet. That was one of the lowest points in my life, but I made it through it. No matter what comes to you, tell yourself that you can handle it. Have you encountered adversity in the past where you have made it through okay? Of course you have! You handled it and you can handle it again when it comes to you in the future. It will always be there and it will never be one hundred percent escapable. You may not be able to always control crappy things that happen to you, but you can handle the way you approach them mentally.

Chapter Eleven Highlights

- ✓ Be more cheerful in everyday life
- ✓ Are you the most important person in your life?
- ✓ When you dwell on events from the past, you are taking those problems and all the emotion that went along with them, and bringing them back into your life in the present.
- ✓ Learn from past experiences and only hold on to emotions that serve you
- ✓ Your mind is not you. It's a separate entity that doesn't define you and won't define you unless you let it.
- ✓ Most of the things you worry about never end up happening.
- ✓ Three steps to overcoming worry: Ask yourself what's the worst that could happen, accept that it is a possible outcome, and then focus on improving on it.

- ✓ Live in the present moment. Act as if you have chosen your life just as it is right now
- ✓ Be conscious of the voice in your head always feeding you negative crap and tell it to shut the f&@k up!
- ✓ Fear and worry are both the anticipation of something negative. Meaning, you are not present.
- ✓ Take notice of all the beautiful things that surround you every day.
- ✓ Avoid the Three Killer R's – Resentment, Regret, and Reacting
- ✓ No matter what comes your way in life, always tell yourself you can handle it!

BONUS CHAPTER

UNDERSTANDING ONLINE DATING

In recent years online dating has become a mainstream way of meeting people. It's just that now it doesn't have the same stigma that it used to. At one time, people would do anything to avoid telling others they had to go online just to meet someone! Things certainly have evolved since the days of the old personal ads.

If you are still unsure about trying online dating, then you have to ask yourself why. There are many reasons why more and more people are flocking over to it. Some people have busy schedules that don't line up with meeting people through traditional methods. Others are tired of the bar scene and are curious about exploring other options. In today's world, online dating has just become another great way of meeting people. If you are serious about finding someone, then there is no reason not to have an online dating profile. After all, why would you not want to explore every possible option to find Mr. Right? Leave no stone unturned! He may very well be on one of these dating sites looking for you right now. So what are you waiting for? Get past any apprehension you had towards online dating right now and register a profile to get started.... And make sure you take this seriously!

A warning before we get started.... online dating can be frustrating in its own way. It can eat up hours of your time, and the online world is filled men who are just looking for sex. There are however a multitude of great men out there who are also using online dating. Men who are very serious about finding the love of their life, and settling down. Great men who would love to meet, and get to know YOU!

I'm going to take you through the steps of getting set up with online dating in a way that will differentiate you from all the other women out there. By positioning yourself in a unique way, you gain an advantage over your competition.

GETTING STARTED WITH ONLINE DATING

Many dating sites will let you do some limited browsing before even registering an account, so go ahead and take a poke around and see which one appeals to you the most. Some sites are free, while others have monthly access fees. Some of the free sites include pof.com and okcupid.com. Some of the paid sites are match.com, lavalife.com and eharmony.com. You can have success on all of them and I suggest trying out the free sites first to get a feel for how the whole concept works. You may find the paid sites have a smaller pool of desirable men, but you may get people who are a little more serious on a site like e-harmony, which is more relationship focused.

YOUR HEADLINE

Once you have selected a dating site and open an account, you'll then fill out your profile. This usually starts with some sort of opening line or headline. The headline is typically displayed alongside your picture, where members will see it as soon as they click to view your profile. If a guy likes the way you look in your picture, he is going to click on it regardless of what you say in your opener. You could say something ridiculous like 'I like meatballs' and he will still click on it, it doesn't matter. This is why your picture is the most important factor in getting him to click on your profile. However, if he is 'borderline' as to whether he wants to check you out or not, then that is where a cleverly thought up headline can work wonders.

Your goal here is to draw some attention by using something witty or eye catching. The more creative and fun you can be with it, the better your profile looks overall. There are a few different styles you can try out that will give you an edge over all the boring subject lines of your competition.

Here are some great examples:

The cocky & funny headline

"100% Pure Awesomeness. Period."

"Go ahead and click on my profile. You KNOW you want to ;)"

You will no doubt get some hate messages for using these from men saying you are 'conceited'. These are not the men you want anyway. Delete and block (more on hate messages later).

The 'playful attack on your competition' headline

"The girl above me is a gold digger and the girl below me is in prison."

Most online dating sites will list pictures in a column with the headline beside it. The above headline says something negative about the girl both above and below you. Of course, you have no clue which members will be displayed above or below you, which is what makes this headline funny.

The joke headline

"Why do toasters have a setting to burn the toast to the point where no one would eat it?"

"Even at a Mensa convention... someone is the dumbest person in the room"

"If at first you don't succeed, then skydiving isn't for you"

While the joke headline typically will have nothing at all to do with your profile, they can demonstrate that you have a sense of humor, even if the rest of your profile isn't funny.

The prank headline

"Did you know that the word 'gullible' isn't in the dictionary?"

The smarter ones will laugh as they will get it right away. Actually, I'd be curious to know how many guys actually email you and tell you that you're wrong. At least you will get an idea of their intellectual level right from the start!

The 'don't tempt me' headline

"DON'T click on my profile or you will suffer the consequences!"

It's only human nature that after reading this headline, they won't be able to resist checking you out!

The 'men's interest' headline

"Bring on the beer!"

"Beer and football – Need I say more?"

Anything that appeals to men will make you seem 'cool' in our eyes and is enough to put a smile on our faces. Of course, if you are going to use a men's interest headline, make sure it is something that you at least have a little interest, as he will no doubt ask you about it later.

WHAT TO SAY IN YOUR PROFILE

Keep in mind, men are always going to look at your picture first, and will often make their initial decision to contact you based on that alone. But that doesn't mean you don't have to pay close attention to what you write in your profile. I have encountered many beautiful women online where I have loved their pictures, but they bored the heck out of me in their profile, so I didn't make contact. After all, do you want someone who is interested in you just for your looks? Or do you want someone who is interested in your for your striking personality and all the other little fun and cool things about you? I have read many profiles that say something along the lines of "ummm... if there is anything you want to know, just ask!" Of COURSE there are things I want to know! But you shouldn't be expecting me to pry it out of you. You need to show men why they should be asking in the first place. A profile like this is nothing short of lazy, yet I see them all the time. I mentioned earlier to take this seriously, and that means putting some effort into it. Writing an interesting profile isn't always easy (ok, it's never easy), but it's well worth the time and effort. The following are some boring examples I have seen. I'll keep them to a minimum so you don't fall asleep, but you get the idea:

> *"TBD"* (yes, that's it.)
>
> *"Looking to meet someone for dating and possible relationship. Please have a pic or I won't respond."*
>
> *"I value time with family and friends, I'm caring, have strong values, and like movies and long walks on the beach."*

SNOREFEST! There is nothing wrong with mentioning these things in your profile, but do it in a fun and playful way that shows the boys why you're different. There are so many profiles I see that are only two or three boring lines (or even just a few words). You don't want to write a whole book either, as no one will read it. Two or three well written paragraphs of average length are fine (about a half to three quarters of a page of text). Paragraphs should be kept a little shorter when writing a profile as it makes them much easier to read online.

Your profile should have a friendly and fun vibe. Men will LOVE profiles that make them laugh, just as you like theirs when they do the same. You don't have to be Ellen Degeneres, but try to use a bit of humor wherever possible. It can even be something cheesy and stupid that most people won't find funny. Who cares, as long as it makes you smile while getting your personality across. Write it in a way that is entertaining to YOU. It doesn't even have to be funny. It just has to be a little different from the barrage of bore that most people have on their profiles.

If you want guys to message you with something better than 'hi' then give them something to message you about. Make sure there is something in your profile they can work with! Anything that's a little different will get a positive response.

Here's an example of my most successful profile:

Headline:

AVAILABLE – One, Caucasian male, slightly used, but in great shape. Online special only. Act NOW!

Body:

PRODUCT INFORMATION:

This package contains 1 energetic, spontaneous, adventurous, and playful guy. This particular top-of-the-line model has a great sense of humor, is self-employed and is equipped with the 'career stability' upgrade.

Specific uses: Boating, sailing, waterskiing, fishing, cottaging, camping, jetskiing, scuba diving, downhill skiing, snowmobiling, hiking, reading, working out, sexual gratification or anything outdoors. Especially good for anything around water. Great for indoor use also.

Item may be used with someone who is compatible with qualities listed above. Some similar interests may be required.

This item is fluent in two languages: English and sarcasm (WARNING: If you cannot handle a sarcastic sense of humor, you may not be compatible with this item)

Lifetime warranty - Item may be returned at anytime if not completely satisfied.

Package includes style and comes complete with nice shoes and nice teeth ;)

Self-maintenance program included. This product can be found at the gym 5 days per week.

WARNING!!!!!!!! - This item can be very addictive. A wacky & sarcastic sense of humor may be required.

Limited quantity available (ummm... just one actually).

Not valid or to be used with any other offer.

Contact for complete details.

Ideal first date (plentyoffish.com): Ummm... lets see. I figured we would go to McDonalds so I can show you how many cheeseburgers I can stuff in my mouth at once. That's usually a big hit with the ladies. :P

If anyone reading my profile didn't get the sarcasm in the last line, then they wouldn't be for me anyway. I had fun writing it and it made me laugh.

I received more compliments on that profile than any other profile I have written. Why? It's completely different from everything else out there. While it is not rip-roaringly funny, it has a bit of humor included that makes most people smile when they read it. It has all that otherwise 'boring' stuff in there as well, but its presented in a fun and interesting way.

AVOID NEGATIVE PROFILES

I used to see these profiles ALL the time! 'Please don't message me if you are this, that or the other thing.' It goes on and on. If your entire profile is negative, then how is that demonstrating that you would be fun and interesting to get to know? You'll just come off as a grouch. I can understand that online dating can be frustrating with the barrage of boring losers you will get messaging you every day… but that doesn't excuse you from having an interesting profile. You want your profile to actually attract the person you WANT, or you're just defeating the purpose of being online in the first place. Yes, you will get a lot of losers messaging you. It's inevitable. But you'll be able to weed most of them out right away, and delete them. No response needed. Never feel like you have to be nice and respond to everyone that messages you. You don't. It's okay to include who you don't want to message you, but that should be just a short part of your profile (and not in your opening line! Can you say, 'grouch?') **Most guys messaging you won't be reading your profile at first anyway, so don't turn off the quality men who actually do care about who you are and what you have to say.** You may turn away some of the men you don't want, but you'll be turning away most of the men you do.

YOUR PICTURES

Once you get your profile written, you'll want to choose some pictures to put up, including one profile picture. The profile picture is the first thing men will see, and is what will help them to decide whether to actually look at your profile or just move on to the next one, so you want to make it a great shot! Professional pictures are okay too, as long as you include non-professional pictures as well. That way, men will know you are a real person and didn't just clip them out of a magazine.

When you don't have a profile picture, men don't know WHO they are even talking to. For all they know, they could be talking to another guy (and sometimes, they probably are). People lie and exaggerate online. It's pretty rampant, as everyone wants to 'sell' themselves. This applies to both men and women. It's pretty easy to bend the truth, or flat out lie, which makes pictures all that much more important.

A single picture isn't good enough either. I went out on dates with women who looked fantastic from the single picture they posted, but when I met them in person they looked absolutely nothing like their picture. It happens with both men and women. Make sure you put up a lot of pictures, so he has a good idea of what you actually look like. It's fine to use that one great shot of yourself where the light is hitting you just right, but just make sure there are other more realistic pictures of yourself as well. This way, potential suitors will have a good idea of what to expect when they meet you. You are just setting yourself up for disappointment otherwise. Never misrepresent yourself online as nothing good can come of it.

Stella, a bisexual friend of mine went online to meet another girl. It didn't take her long before she met Teri. They spent hours chatting online, but never actually spoke before finally agreeing to meet up at a local coffee shop. Teri seemed to be late, but Stella noticed a strange man sitting a few tables over who kept looking over at her. She thought to herself... "PLEASE tell me that's not who I came here to meet!" The man got up and walked over to her. "Stella? Hi, it's 'Terry'. I'm really sorry, but I didn't think you would want to meet me otherwise." Her fears were confirmed. She stood up, pissed off and in utter disbelief that this actually happened. She stormed out without saying a word.

This is an extreme example, but demonstrates why you want to show more pictures and why you should pay more interest to profiles with lots of pictures as well.

You also want to have a wide variety of pictures, rather than just putting up all headshots or selfies. If he sees all selfies, he is going to wonder if you even have any friends! Pictures of you doing fun things are always good. Have a shot of yourself in front of the pyramids in Egypt? Use it. Have a pic of yourself feeding an elephant? Use it. Have a picture of yourself doing a flip while wakeboarding? Use it! Pictures are great for demonstrating the fun and interesting things you like to do. They tell the story much better than simply saying it in your profile, so use them to your advantage! They also give men a reason to message you and gives them something to comment on. It makes it all that much easier for them to send you something interesting that could lead to a connection. Otherwise, if you have a boring profile and no interesting pictures, then even the man who is otherwise perfect for you may stuggle to find something unique and original to say in his message. After all, if you aren't coming across as unique and original in your profile or in your pictures, then how is he supposed to come up with an original and interesting message for you?

Even if you don't have a picture up, you will no doubt still get some messages from men, however significantly fewer. If you happen to be in a line of work where you can't make your picture visible in your profile, then make sure you give a detailed description of yourself. You want to explain why you aren't showing your picture so anyone reading will understand. Tell them that there are pictures available that can be released on request. You of course don't have to release them to ANYONE until you feel comfortable. If you are physically attractive, then don't be afraid to mention that. If you are concerned about sounding conceited than you can always say something like, "others say I'm attractive", and leave it at that. If some men don't like it, then too bad for them. If you don't consider yourself physically attractive (and everyone is beautiful in their own way) then you have to show them how great you are in your profile.

You also want to ensure your pictures are recent. You aren't making it any easier on yourself by showing a picture of yourself at 28 when you are now 38. And don't try to justify it either by saying something like, "well, I still look like that". Trust me, you don't. You may 'resemble' that, but that isn't who you are anymore. Would you want to waste time meeting up with a guy who posted pictures that were 10 years old? Make sure your pictures are no more than a year old, and it doesn't hurt to mention that in your profile as well. That way, men will know they are looking at current images.

YOUR INTENTION STATUS

Most dating websites will have a category to select the type of relationship you are looking for from a drop down menu. The options vary from one site to the next, but are typically very similar to this:

- Relationship
- Casual dating
- Wants to date but nothing serious
- Isn't seeking commitment
- Casual sex
- Marriage

Relationship

It should sound obvious that anyone making this selection would be looking for a relationship. It is unlikely that a man looking for only sex would select this option. But just because he has 'relationship' selected as his intention, it doesn't mean that he won't be open to casual sex as well. He may ultimately want a relationship, but that doesn't necessarily mean he won't message just for sex. For example, some women will put up very sexy, scantily clad pictures of themselves and then select the 'relationship' option. While these pictures will get A LOT of attention from men online, you will capture a lot of attention from men just looking for sex… regardless of whether they say they are looking for a serious relationship or not. It doesn't matter whether you mention you aren't looking to 'hook up' or not either, as there are some men who just don't care. You can still easily eliminate these men by putting off sex with them or hinting that you will be putting off sex with them as I explained in detail in Chapter Ten. Even if you say in your profile that you're not interested in flings and guys just looking for sex, this won't stop them from messaging you. You may deter some, but definitely not all. Always be on your guard, regardless of how comfortable he may make you feel.

Casual Dating

If you are serious about finding a relationship, then you want to make sure you choose the relationship option and not casual dating. It implies that you aren't sure what you are looking for and that you could just be looking for sex. It's more neutral, and can be taken either way. It's a good option to select if you haven't made up your mind as to what you want. A lot of men however will take this as an open invitation to message you for sex. I find many of the women selecting this option really are looking for relationships, but they are receiving a larger number of inquiries from men just interested in sex.

If the guy has 'casual dating' selected, then this is what I would call a 'proceed with caution' selection. It could mean that he is only looking for sex, but wants to keep his options open. A guy with 'casual dating' selected as his intention can still easily message women looking for a relationship OR a woman who is looking for casual sex and it won't come across as strange or unusual either way. It's just neutral, and would most likely be the setting of any guy who has commitment issues. You really need to keep your guard up when considering someone with 'casual dating' selected.

Wants to date but nothing serious

To men, selecting this option implies you are looking for sex and you will get a larger pool of men messaging you for this reason, thinking that this is what you want. I still see many women selecting this as their intention, but then saying they are looking for a relationship, either in their profile, or once communication has begun. If a guy has this option selected, then assume he is looking for sex. Don't initiate or engage in any kind of contact with a man with this status unless you too are looking for a fling, as it is unlikely it will lead anywhere else.

Isn't seeking a relationship or any kind of commitment

This option means exactly what it says, yet women looking for relationships will still message guys with this status. Anyone with this option selected should be looking for only sex, or for a 'friend with benefits'. That is, a friend who you have sex with on occasion, but have no interest in having a relationship with.

Casual sex

Just like with 'isn't seeking a relationship or any kind of commitment', this one should be self explanatory. Just a bit more blatant about it. If you are just looking for sex, and don't care who knows about it, then this is the option for you. If a guy has this selected, don't expect it to go any further than sex.

Marriage

While this may ultimately be what you want, don't select this under any circumstances. I'm not even sure why it is listed as an option as it just comes across as needy and desperate. No one is looking for marriage first. You look for the relationship first, then marriage. I'd be hesitant to message a woman with this setting regardless of how badly I wanted to settle down.

BODY TYPE

This is where you are going to select your body type, so whoever is reading your profile knows what to expect when he meets you. Just like the status of what you are looking for, the exact wording varies from one site to the next, but the context is all the same. The options usually look something like this:

- Slim
- Average

- A few extra pounds
- Full-figured / big and beautiful
- Athletic
- Muscular

This is usually where women lie the most (where men lie most about their height). In fact, I find that most women who are overweight (but not obese) will select 'average' as their body type. I have even seen some very large women selecting 'average' when you can see quite clearly in their pictures they are not. Keep in mind, some men look for and prefer women who are a little heavier, so wouldn't you rather be honest so you can better attract the men who actually want you for who you are? He is going to find out the truth anyway, so why not just be honest up front? At least put some pictures up so men can form their own decision on your body type. If you can't be honest with yourself, then how can you expect others to be honest with you? If you truly think you are average, then by all means, select average, but if you think you may be pushing it, then you probably are.

Ryan has been looking for a serious relationship for some time and decided to try out online dating. He quickly meant Shelly and they emailed back and forth for days before deciding to meet. They decided to meet up for drinks and when they did, he immediately noticed Shelly was a lot heavier than he was expecting. While she had a lot of pictures, he remembers they were all just head shots. While he was really looking forward to meeting her and thought they had a connection, he feels she misrepresented herself online. He cut the date short saying that he had some work to take care of. Shelly never heard from him again.

Even if Ryan was open to meeting someone who has a few extra pounds they would like to get rid of, the misrepresentation is hard to get past for anyone. You wouldn't want to date a guy who says he is six feet tall and you meet him and he is five-foot-six. It's the same thing (and happens often).

It's important to be honest with online dating as you are only setting yourself up for disappointment later. I have female friends who have gone on dates with men they have met online where their pictures showed them with a full head of hair. Then when they met, they were as bald as an eagle! You are online to find people you will one day meet up with. They are going to find out the truth sooner or later, so don't waste your time, or theirs.

WHEN TO MEET

It's important that you feel comfortable before agreeing to meet someone you met online. I have found some women will want to meet up fairly quickly while others might take weeks or sometimes even months before feeling comfortable enough to meet up. Keep in mind that online dating, email, texting and even talking on the phone is NOT the real world. Just because you have a connection this way, doesn't necessarily mean you are going to have one when you meet up in person. It's all about chemistry, and it is something that has to be felt when the two of you are physically present with one another. This is exactly why you don't want to wait too long before meeting up. Until you meet face to face, you really don't know if you are wasting your time or not.

Once initial contact has been made, you will naturally email each other back and forth on the site. If you feel there is some potential, perfect. Exchange numbers and switch to texting. Now you have to see if you can maintain the same chemistry. If you can keep it going, the next step will be to speak on the phone. Sometimes people clam up on the phone and the chemistry might not be the same as it were if you were hiding behind your computer or your device. Once you feel confident you have chemistry on the phone (and this can be after a single phone call) then you'll want to meet up and see if you have the same chemistry in person.

THE ONLINE DATING SEQUENCE

This whole online dating sequence can quite often fall apart at this stage, which is why I suggest meeting up quickly.

Jacqueline and Steven were really hitting it off online. They texted each other regularly and even spoke on the phone a few times per week. They both felt like they had found their soul mate, but Jaqueline was still very apprehensive about meeting people online. After a month, she finally decided to meet with him. To both of their surprise, they had very little to say to each other. The same connection they felt on the phone and via text was non-existent in person. To Jacqueline, Steven seemed like a completely different person. Since she felt so strongly connected with him before they met, she thought she would give it one more try. Unfortunately, the way she felt did not improve the second time around. She sent him a long email saying how she just wasn't feeling anything more than friendship toward him, however she was just being polite. She didn't want anything to do with him after that.

The story of Jacqueline and Steven happens frequently. Sometimes people don't show their true colors until you have met them face to face. In the above story, Jacqueline was the one who lost interest in Steven after meeting him, but it can also work the other way just as easily.

WHERE TO MEET

Your first meeting should be something fairly simple and inexpensive. Don't look at the guy as being cheap if he just suggests going for coffee on the first meeting. Notice how I say 'first meeting' and not 'first date'. Your goal here should not be to have an official 'date', but to size each other up to ensure you are both who you said you were, and that your initial connection is maintained. If things look good and you both like each other, it can always be converted to a date. Committing to a dinner or even to drinks can get pretty expensive for a guy when trying to find his dream woman online. Besides, if you meet up with someone who isn't who he said he was, do you really want to be stuck with him for an hour or more over dinner?

Now, if he invites you out for coffee for a 'real date' after he has already met you, then I agree that's cheap.

ONLINE SAFETY

Whenever meeting men online, it is crucially important to remember that this is the internet, and there are some whackos out there. Regardless of what pictures he has on his profile, or how nice and friendly he comes across, you still have no idea who this person actually is. How do you know he didn't just cut and paste every single one of his pictures from someone else's profile? You really have no idea. I very recently had someone steal a bunch of my pictures and used them to set up a Facebook profile. I was really lucky that one of my Facebook friends found out about it and tipped me off. If it has happened to me, than I am pretty sure it happens all the time. This further proves that you have no idea who you are talking to until you actually meet.

When you decide to meet up with someone, always make sure you are in a public place such as a busy coffee shop, restaurant, or mall. Never have him pick you up and always meet him there! In fact, I don't recommend getting into his car at all on the first meeting. Anyone can put on a front and pretend to be someone they are not, and some people are quite good at it. Always keep your personal safety in mind.

I have a friend who meets women online regularly and for their first meeting, he invites them over to his place. While he is completely harmless, the women who oblige have no idea who he is. I'm astonished at how many women actually accept his invitation. I can't even begin to tell you how big of a risk they are taking.

WHAT TO EXPECT FROM MEN ONLINE

There are some particularly attractive women who can literally receive over one hundred messages per day. Most of these however, can be eliminated almost immediately. An equally attractive man will not have anywhere near the same experience, and might get five or six messages per day from women. Just like with women, most of his messages can be eliminated immediately. Most guys who are even slightly attractive however, might receive only one or two messages per week, if any at all. No matter how attractive the guy is, how well his profile is written and how clever his message is to you, he may only receive response on 30% of the messages he sends. But that is only if he really has his stuff together with looks, profile, and multiple pictures of himself doing fun things and having a good time. 30% however is EXTREMELY high for most men, even attractive men of high value. A half decent looking man with an average to even slightly above average profile will be doing well if he gets a 10% response rate on messages sent.

For this reason, some men may send you either dull or 'cut and paste' messages initially. It could be something like any of the following:

- Hi
- Hello
- How are you today?
- What are you up to?
- How are you finding this site?

Pretty boring right? Now some men truly are this boring and don't really have anything more to say. But if they look half decent from their pictures, take a look at their profiles and make a decision as to whether you want to message them back from there. If you don't think a guy sounds particularly interesting, then just delete his message. No need to respond. But if he sounds like he could be fun or someone you might connect with from his profile, then why not send him a quick message back? You can then see what he can come up with in his second message when he knows he has your interest. He will no doubt say a lot more in the second message than he did in the first. Especially if you have given him something to work with, either in your profile or in your response.

Some men will message you with something clever or witty that is a little more generic and can be 'cut and paste' and sent out to multiple women. While this doesn't sound particularly appealing at first, if it sounds relatively good, then check out his profile anyway. Don't eliminate a guy for this, especially if it was pretty good. Remember, his response ratio is most likely going to be well below 30%, which is why he is doing this. Message him back and see if his second message matches the same wit, creativity or energy level.

I used to spend twenty or thirty minutes (or longer) reading profiles and carefully writing the perfect opening message to every woman I wanted to talk to. Some of the stuff I came up with was pure gold! (Of course!) However much to my disappointment, the response rate was still dismal when compared with the amount of effort that went into each one. I stopped doing that pretty fast once I saw my return on the time invested. This is why so many men don't bother to read your profile the first time (or will just give it a quick skim through). He'll read it once you message him back and knows that you are at least slightly interested. Some people get pretty busy and online dating can be extremely time consuming.

While there are some rather boring messages you will receive that I suggest you shouldn't eliminate immediately, there are many that you will want to hit the delete button without even looking at his profile. I have posted some of the more common messages sent by 'men' below, as told to me by some of my female friends. I've added my comments following each one. For those already familiar with the online dating scene, these should give you a good laugh as I'm sure you can relate:

- *-how r u 2 day* (Apparently he thinks it is quite the time commitment to spell out a few three letter words in full.)

- *i jist wanned too tel u that i licked yor pofil an waz hopin i cud chatt with u somtim hop to heer frum u* (I think what this fine young man was trying to say, is "I just wanted to tell you that I liked your profile and was hoping we could chat sometime. Hope to hear from you." He can't spell and doesn't understand what punctuation or capital letters are for. Really? In a world with spell check, there is no excuse.)

- *You are a gorgeous fox! Will you marry me?* (I think this guy would actually take you up on it if you said yes.)

- -*Whaaaaazzzzzaaaaaaaapp!!!!* (Why anyone still thinks this is funny or would be a good opening message is beyond me. Actually, why anyone ever thought it was funny is beyond my comprehension.)

- *I must have died and gone to heaven! Your SOOO hot! Wanna F*&K?* (Seriously buddy? I can't imagine this working even with women who are only looking for sex.).

It blows my mind that so many men can't come up with anything better than the above. This is exactly why I say most of the messages you receive can be deleted easily. Don't get frustrated if you are getting an excessive amount of messages from losers. Just follow my guidelines as mentioned above and you should be able to filter through them fairly and pick out the real gems while eliminating the trash.

HATERS

Keep in mind that when you are dealing with online dating, you are going to have every loser, virgin, and clueless man out there online as well. They can't meet women in real life, so what other options do they have?

You will encounter some very weak men that may send you hate messages when you don't respond to them. They can be flat out mean sometimes and will call you selfish, conceited, into yourself or may call you even more hurtful names. Never take any crap or lack of respect from men online! Don't ever let it bother you as their hate message is 100% about their lack of self confidence and self esteem and has absolutely NOTHING to do with you. They are just trying to protect their highly fragile little egos and lashing out helps them to deal with the rejection (yes, they need serious help). Just smile and laugh about it and try to enjoy it for its entertainment value. The only real meaning it has is the meaning that YOU give it.

No matter how bad the hate message may be, just delete it and block the loser. I have a friend who received a nasty hate message after only five minutes! He saw that she had opened the message from him and when he didn't hear back immediately, he fired back with hate. Unbelievable, and I truly feel sorry for this guy.

MESSAGING GUYS FIRST

If you feel that you are getting inundated with messages from men and you want to have more control over your inbox, then there is an option for that too. Most sites will allow you to make your profile invisible to everyone but those you have corresponded with. This allows you to do the search and to find the men that interest you the most. Keep in mind this can be extremely time consuming, but if you find you are getting frustrated with all the messages from losers, then this is a great way for you to take back some control.

As discussed in Chapter Six, don't get yourself into a situation where you are chasing him. Always let men do the chasing. Deep down, this is what we all want. While it is nice for us to have women throwing themselves at us, it's unlikely it will lead to a serious and lasting relationship unless you let him take the reigns.

BONUS CHAPTER SUMMARY

- ✓ Get some attention with a witty or creative headline that stands out from the rest.
- ✓ Make your profile interesting. Many desirable men will overlook a boring profile.
- ✓ Avoid really short or really long profiles. Length should be about ½ to ¾ of a page.
- ✓ Keep paragraphs shorter as they are easier to read online.
- ✓ Avoid profiles that are full of negativity. They will turn off 'some' of the men you don't want, but 'all' of the men you do.
- ✓ Your profile picture is the first thing men will see, so make it a good one.
- ✓ Have multiple pictures of you doing fun and interesting things
- ✓ Setting your intention status to 'casual' or 'nothing serious' will attract a lot more men only looking for sex.
- ✓ Be honest about your body type. This is where most women lie (most men lie about their height).
- ✓ When you find someone you like, meet up fairly quickly. It isn't the real world until you meet face to face.
- ✓ Always meet up in a public place. Put your safety first!
- ✓ Your first 'meeting' is not a date. You are just sizing each other up and making sure you can connect in the real world. Meeting up for coffee is perfect.

- ✓ While some women get inundated with messages, even the most attractive and desirable man won't be.
- ✓ Most men will get a very low response rate on their messages sent.
- ✓ A dull message from a man doesn't necessarily mean he is dull. If his picture looks good, check out his profile and make your decision from there.
- ✓ Never let a mean or hurtful message from a guy you don't know bother you. It's 100% about their lack of self-confidence and poor self-esteem and has nothing to do with you personally.
- ✓ If you are getting too many messages, then you can hide your profile and only message the guys you are interested in.

CONCLUSION

Everyone deserves to be with the person that is truly suited to them. The world is no doubt full of jerks and losers, but there are also zillions of great men out there and there is a great one out there for you. Don't ever settle for anyone who is just mediocre, as you deserve much better than that. You deserve to be with someone who is as good as you are.

Make sure you commit to following the material in this book and be sure to continue to use it for reference. It is important to start putting it to work right way as the longer you wait, the greater the chance you will never put it to use. The journey is not always easy and it isn't always fun, but you have to make the best of it as it comes to you. Often when you look back at parts of your life that you thought were crappy, some of them may not have been as bad as you made them out to be at the time.

Whatever happened in the past is over and done with. Your new approach to dating starts now. Put a big smile on your face knowing that the best is yet to come. Know that Mr. Right is out there looking for YOU right now as well, and he may very well be just around the corner.

ABOUT THE AUTHOR

Having been a serial dater for over 15 years, Paul J. Meredith has been through the dating trenches. He went from not being able to get a date to the point where dating became an addiction. During this time, Paul noticed many patterns and mistakes that were common among women. These patterns were holding them back from finding the right person and were opening them up to being used and hurt. He realized it didn't have to be this way. If these women had some guidance, they could significantly increase their dating success by weeding out all the guys that were just wasting their time.

Paul has been 'officially' studying male-female interactions and early stages of relationships since 2005. His knowledge base is comprised of life lessons combined with years of studying social dynamics. He has been to many seminars, bootcamps, and has read countless books on dating written for both men and women. Now a dating coach, Paul is passionate about helping women to understand the way men think, as well as to better understand their own thoughts and actions.

He currently resides in Toronto, Canada where he lives a

healthy and active lifestyle. When he's not spending time at the gym, you can often find him enjoying his other passion – sailing, as well as spending time with his family, friends and his long-term girlfriend Kelly. Paul is also involved in modelling and acting, which allows not only for his creative side to come out, but also as a great way to meet new people.

Visit his blog at www.pauljmeredith.com